CAMPAIGN • 213

# IRELAND 1649–52

## Cromwell's Protestant Crusade

**MICHAEL McNALLY**      ILLUSTRATED BY GRAHAM TURNER

*Series editors* Marcus Cowper and Nikolai Bogdanovic

First published in Great Britain in 2009 by Osprey Publishing,
Midland House, West Way, Botley, Oxford OX2 0PH, UK
443 Park Avenue South, New York, NY 10016, USA
E-mail: info@ospreypublishing.com

A CIP catalogue record for this book is available from the British Library.

ISBN: 978 1 84603 368 1
E-book ISBN: 978 1 84908 087 3

Editorial by Ilios Publishing Ltd, Oxford, UK (www.iliospublishing.com)
Page layout by: The Black Spot
Index by Auriol Griffith-Jones
Typeset in Sabon and Myriad Pro
Maps by Bounford.com
3D bird's-eye views by The Black Spot
Battlescene illustrations by Graham Turner
Originated by PPS Grasmere Ltd
Printed in China through Worldprint

09  10  11  12  13     10 9 8 7 6 5 4 3 2 1

## AUTHOR'S NOTE

As always, I'd like to thank my wife – Petra – and children – Stephen, Elena
and Liam – for their forbearance and understanding throughout the whole
time in which I was working on this project. It has been an exceptionally
difficult year, and they were always there for me.

I'd also like to take this opportunity to thank several people whose
contributions have been crucial – firstly my editor, Marcus Cowper,
for his support during the bad times and his patience during the final
stages; Andy Copestake and Lee Offen for proofreading the manuscript
for me; Seán Ó Brógáin both for his excellent artwork and for sharing
his knowledge of the period with me; Dr David Murphy of the NUI in
Maynooth for his continued encouragement and support; Kieran Laffan
for kindly agreeing to photograph many of the sites associated with
Cromwell's southern campaign; and Thomas Brogan for driving me
halfway across Ireland at the drop of a hat so that I could visit Drogheda
and the Mill Mount.

Finally I'd like to thank Izabel Pennec-Murphy (OPW Ireland), Louise Morgan
(NGI Dublin), Helen Trompeteler (NPG Lodon), Savenna Donohue (Cavan
County Museum, Ballyjamesduff, Co. Cavan), Betty Quinn and Noel Bailey
(Millmount Museum, Drogheda, Co. Louth), and Michael Gilroy-Sinclair
(Royal Armouries, Leeds) for their assistance in sourcing a number of
images for reproduction in the book.

## ARTIST'S NOTE

Readers may care to note that the original paintings from which the colour
plates in this book were prepared are available for private sale. The
Publishers retain all reproduction copyright whatsoever. All enquiries
should be addressed to:

Graham Turner, PO Box 568, Aylesbury, Buckinghamshire, HP17 8ZK, UK

The Publishers regret that they can enter into no correspondence upon
this matter.

## THE WOODLAND TRUST

Osprey Publishing are supporting the Woodland Trust, the UK's leading
woodland conservation charity, by funding the dedication of trees.

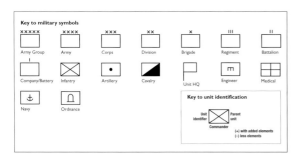

FOR A CATALOGUE OF ALL BOOKS PUBLISHED BY OSPREY MILITARY
AND AVIATION PLEASE CONTACT:

Osprey Direct, c/o Random House Distribution Center,
400 Hahn Road, Westminster, MD 21157
Email: uscustomerservice@ospreypublishing.com

Osprey Direct, The Book Service Ltd, Distribution Centre,
Colchester Road, Frating Green, Colchester, Essex, CO7 7DW
E-mail: customerservice@ospreypublishing.com

www.ospreypublishing.com

# CONTENTS

# The coming of the Lord Deputy, January–August 1649

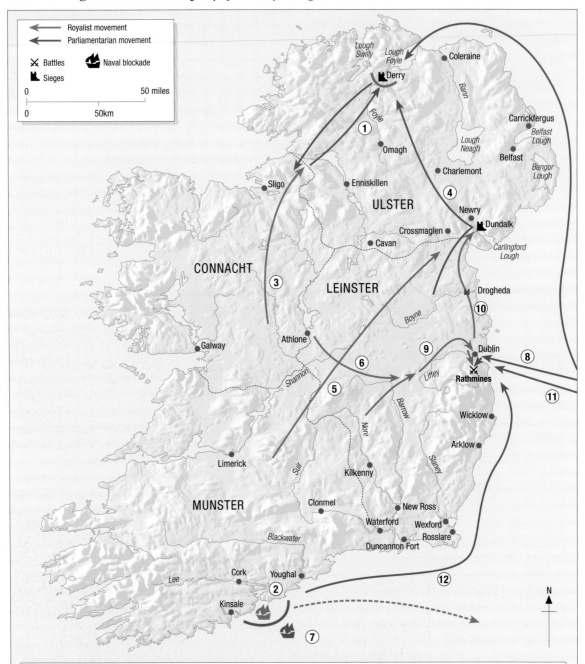

1. January: Sir Charles Coote launches a pre-emptive raid into Northern Connacht in order to destroy the Royalists's supplies and reduce their offensive capability. On his return to Derry the city is besieged by the protestant Laggan Army.
2. January: Royalist warships under Prince Rupert assemble at Kinsale and begin operations against Parliamentarian shipping.
3. In order to prevent Ó Neill from moving into Connacht, Clanricarde moves a blocking force to Ballinasloe.
4. March: forsaking the Catholic Confederacy and, outnumbered by the combined forces of Inchiquin and Castlehaven, Ó Neill moves back into Ulster. En route he enters into agreements with the Parliamentarian garrisons of Dundalk and Derry, his arrival at the latter forcing the Lagganeers to break off the siege.
5. The Earl of Castlehaven begins operations against Ó Neill garrisons in Leinster.
6. June: Coalition forces under Ormond and Inchiquin converge before joining forces for a march on Dublin
7. 22 May: Robert Blake, Parliamentarian general-at-sea, arrives off Kinsale with a large naval squadron and blockades the port, thereby removing any threat to the proposed transfer of troops to Ireland.
8. The advance guard of Cromwell's Army (two regiments of foot and one of horse) under the command of John Reynolds lands in Dublin on 22 July to reinforce Michael Jones's Army. Two companies from Huncks's regiment of foot sail directly to reinforce Coote in Derry.
9. July: Ormond commences operation to capture Dublin and establishes his headquarters at Finglas north of the city. On 1 August he re-crosses the Liffey and sets up camp at Rathmines. Jones sallies out on 2 August, decisively defeating the coalition army
10. Inchiquin detached with 4,000 men to capture Trim, Drogheda and Dundalk.
11. The main body of Cromwell's Army lands at the port of Ringsend near Dublin on 15 August.
12. Having failed to secure a landing on the Munster coast, the remainder of Cromwell's forces – under Henry Ireton – arrive in Dublin on 23 August.

# ORIGINS OF THE CAMPAIGN

Despite the bitter cold, a crowd had already gathered in the early morning darkness, and, as the sun rose, shadowing a line of troops that had been deployed to keep order, in front of the Banqueting House at Whitehall, the dark mass of a scaffold began to take shape. Draped in swathes of black velvet it stood there, in its centre a headsman's block, a silent portent of the day to come.

Shortly before 10.00am, the sharp staccato rattle of drums echoed along the roadway as a column of soldiers approached from the direction of St James's Palace, opening ranks as they reached Whitehall, allowing a number of men to enter the building and then moving to reinforce the security cordon.

At about noon, a small body of men, both military and civilian, ascended the scaffold preceding a small, slight man wearing a blue cape, the prisoner. Doffing the cape, the man then removed his outer garments and allowed his hair to be placed in a knitted woollen cap. Turning, he addressed a few words to those assembled on the scaffold before kneeling and, arms outstretched, placed his head on the block.

With a nod from the senior officer present, the headsman took up position raising his axe and then, following an almost imperceptible signal from the

Aimed at countering the growing cult surrounding the death of King Charles I, this cartoon from the 1650s shows the king's execution in a scurrilous light, particularly with the headsman's assistant ready to catch the head before it can roll away. (Courtesy Bettmann-Corbis, SF 1364)

The Benburb campaign, summer 1646. Here we see a unit of Scots horse about to launch a charge against Confederate foot. Notice should be made of the distinctive tight woollen trews and short jackets or shirts worn by the Irish troops, as well as the unique 'bodkin'-style pike heads on their primary armament, which would have had no problem punching through cavalry armour. (Courtesy Seán Ó Brógáin)

kneeling man, the blade descended. His office fulfilled, the executioner bent down and took hold of the severed head, lifting it up for the crowd to view, but instead of the jeers and cheers with which Londoners would normally accompany a public execution, a low moan rose up as the crowd recoiled from the sight of the disembodied visage of Charles Stuart, King of England, Scotland and Ireland, soon to be known as Charles the Martyr.

Above the scaffold and from the windows of Whitehall Palace a number of men looked down dispassionately at the final moments of the king that they had consigned to the headsman's axe, aware that if they were to consolidate their hold of the Stuart kingdoms they would need to defeat the only remaining enclave of Royalist support in the British Isles, and put down a rebellion that had begun even before they themselves had risen up in arms.

From the outset of the 17th century, the English Government maintained its control over Ireland by a harsh colonial policy, known as 'plantation', by which Irish landowners were dispossessed and their holdings handed over or sold to Protestant settlers whose loyalty to the Crown would, it was intended, facilitate governmental rule. The process followed a predictable cycle, with discontent and rebellion against the Crown being punished by further dispossessions, which then became the source of further unrest.

These practices were refined during the late 1630s when Sir Thomas Wentworth, Lord Lieutenant of Ireland, began to use the revenue generated as a means to service the royal debt, thus reducing the king's reliance on Parliament. Indeed, many believed that following his elevation to the peerage as earl of Strafford, Wentworth would unleash a further series of confiscations. However, neither he nor they had reckoned with his numerous enemies at Westminster who had him impeached on the vague charge of his 'having committed gross misdemeanours'. Any thoughts that the king may have had of saving his favourite were soon dashed when he was given a stark choice, in effect an ultimatum – either sacrifice Strafford to a trial by his peers or face continued Parliamentary opposition.

By the time of Strafford's subsequent execution, and having seen the Scots twice wring concessions from a weak and indecisive monarch, many Irish magnates initially felt that the time of crisis had passed, but further anti-Catholic legislation soon caused many to see their only remaining option as being a show of force similar to that of the Scots. Believing that the Crown lacked the backbone to stand up to organized resistance, they intended to seize back the settled lands and then present a list of demands to the king, relying upon the open rift between Crown and Parliament to force him to the negotiating table.

The plan was simple enough. Beginning on 22 October 1641, they would seize a number of key objectives throughout the country and from this position of relative strength negotiate with the Crown for a resolution of their grievances. The two key areas were entrusted to Sir Phelim Ó Neíll of Kinard who was to lead the insurgents in Ulster and Conor, Lord Maguire, whose task was to capture Dublin and seize the centre of government. With the capital taken, and Ulster neutralized, the rebels felt that the king could only accede to their demands or run the real risk of losing control of Ireland.

Almost immediately the insurrection ran into difficulty. Insufficient men had gathered in Dublin, and the attack was therefore postponed for 24 hours, during which time the plan was betrayed to the authorities and the ringleaders arrested and summarily executed. In Ulster, the opposite was true with almost all of the initial objectives being easily achieved, but Ó Neíll then overplayed his hand by producing a warrant, allegedly signed by the king, which purported to give royal support to the insurgents. Any calm that this document may have engendered was soon shattered as private grievances began to be resolved at sword point and, with violence spiralling out of control, large numbers of civilians were either forcibly evicted from their homes and left to the mercy of the elements or killed out of hand, not only on account of their religion but also in the settlement of personal disputes.

News of the rising spread quickly to London and although the strained relations between them had not yet degenerated into open warfare, it was clear to both king and Parliament that a military solution had to be quickly found. The problem was that, as the recent conflict with Scotland had shown, the English Army was too small and too ill equipped to mount a major campaign. It was therefore agreed that, to bolster the English forces, the Scots would raise a force of 2,500 men specifically for service in Ulster, with their maintenance costs being underwritten by the English Parliament.

Pikeman's armour New Model Army c.1645–50. Although standard equipment at the beginning of the Civil War, by 1649 body armour was gradually being phased out owing to a combination of cost, weight and maintenance. (Courtesy of the Trustees, Royal Armouries, Leeds)

# CONFEDERATION

As order was gradually re-established, it seemed to many observers as if the government was intent on using the rising as an excuse to indiscriminately further the 'plantations'. Battle lines were quickly being drawn with 'English' on one side and 'Irish' on the other, with no distinction being made for political or religious allegiance.

**LEFT**
Flag of the Ulster Confederates 1646–51. Combining the traditional Irish harp with a green background, Éoghan 'Rua' Ó Neíll's standard has become synonymous with the struggle for Ireland and the national identity. (Courtesy Seán Ó Brógáin)

**RIGHT**
Commonwealth standard, c.1649. Although it is unclear whether it was actually issued to a unit in the field this colour, reconstructed from contemporary sources, combines both the cross of St George and the Irish harp, symbolizing the unification of England and Ireland. (Courtesy Seán Ó Brógáin)

One sign of this solidarity was the foundation of the Confederation of Kilkenny, a central assembly that not only formulated general strategy, but more importantly gave potential allies the outward appearance of dealing with a sovereign state. As a result of this, a number of Irish soldiers serving in Continental armies returned home to enlist in the Confederate armies, most prominent amongst them being Thomas Preston and Éoghan 'Rua' Ó Neíll.

Unaware of how the situation in England would soon deteriorate, the Government began to pour resources into Ireland. With the promised Scots Army of 2,500 men soon increased to an unwieldy 10,000 men, a number of large garrisons were established whilst the remainder of the force was organized for service in the field. Overall command of the English forces was then given to James Butler, Earl of Ormond.

During the final months of 1642, an uneasy peace descended upon Ireland, not through any mutual accord reached by the protagonists but rather as a result of the simple expedient that neither side wished to expend their carefully hoarded supplies in a campaign that would yield little or no tangible benefit, and so as the armies went early into winter quarters, both Preston and Ó Neíll saw this as a perfect opportunity to retrain and reorganize their forces. Much was expected of the two émigré generals, but the new campaigning season could not have begun worse for the Confederates.

With its armies heavily defeated in a number of field actions, it looked certain that the Kilkenny Assembly would be a short-lived exercise in political autonomy – Ulster was firmly in the grips of the Scots Army under the command of Major-General Robert Monro, a veteran officer who had seen extensive service in the Swedish Army of King Gustavus Adolphus, whilst Ormond was steadily consolidating his position in Leinster before, presumably, delivering a *coup de grâce* with the capture of the Confederate capital.

Despite this near disaster on both fronts, the Confederate war effort was saved by the one man who had the most to gain from their defeat. Under increasing pressure from Parliamentarian forces in England and Wales, King Charles was desperate to find additional sources of manpower for his armies, and the only logical source of trained reinforcements was Ormond's Army in Ireland. As it was plain to see that no troops could be spared whilst the country was at war, the earl was therefore instructed to come to terms with the Irish rebels and, despite reservations on both sides, a ceasefire was signed by both parties on 15 September 1642.

The repercussions of the armistice were felt almost immediately. Whilst the majority of Confederates were in favour of the treaty, a small but influential faction led by Giovanni Battista Rinuccini, the Papal nuncio, were in favour of the Irish 'going it alone' and founding an independent Catholic state under the aegis of Rome. As has so often been the case in Irish history, this admixture of factionalism fuelled by self-interest split the high command at a critical time, with Ó Neíll and the Ulster troops supporting Rinuccini whilst the remaining provincial forces supported the Assembly .

Although his negotiations with the Confederates would prove to be inordinately lengthy, Ormond was eventually able to send a force of 5,000 men to England, whilst an additional 1,500 Ulster Confederates under the command of Alasdair MacColla were independently sent to support the Royalist war effort in Scotland.

Pikeman's gorget, English c.1650. With the gradual withdrawal of body armour from service, many pikemen were equipped with gorgets designed to protect their shoulder, neck and upper chest. This example is hinged over the left shoulder and fixed with a socket over the right. (Courtesy of the Trustees, Royal Armouries, Leeds)

## THE LORD LIEUTENANT

Following on from the apparent success of the armistice, Ormond was appointed Lord Lieutenant of Ireland, his effective brief now being to maximize Irish military support for the Crown and in order to do this was granted permission to negotiate a formal treaty with the Confederates. This was, of course, easier to propose than to execute as, although his kinship to many of the Irish commissioners should have smoothed the path of negotiation. It was clear that any religious concessions he made to them would also undermine his support amongst the predominantly Protestant Royalists. Despite this, and following lengthy negotiations a treaty was ratified in early 1646, but was almost immediately disavowed by the Confederate Assembly. Aware that his military position was untenable, Ormond entered into discussions with Westminster, and in July 1647 an accord was signed by which Parliament would receive possession of Dublin as well as Drogheda, Dundalk, Trim and a number of other towns under Royalist control, in addition to the remaining 3,000 men that Ormond had under arms at that time, who would also pass over to Parliamentarian command. In return, Parliament would agree to protect the interests of King Charles's loyal subjects against the Irish rebels and, just as importantly, allow Ormond free passage overseas. Thoroughly disillusioned by his negotiations with the Confederates, Ormond is reputed to have explained his actions by stating that he 'preferred English rebels to Irish ones', however a more realistic explanation is that the Dublin magazines contained less than 10 barrels of powder, with no chance of obtaining further supplies. In short, had Ormond prolonged military operations, his powder reserves would have been expended in a matter of minutes at which time he would have had to have thrown himself upon the dubious mercies of his opponents.

9

# AN IRONSIDE FOR IRELAND

Following the ratification of the Ormond Treaty, Colonel Michael Jones was appointed military governor of Dublin and under his direction priority was given to the reconstruction of the city's defences. Once he was satisfied with the construction work, he reorganized the city garrison with a view to creating a mobile strike force to take the war to the enemy.

On 15 July, Preston's Leinster Army took Naas and moved to besiege Trim, an important staging post in any movement against the capital. On 1 August, Jones left Dublin at the head of about 4,000 men and, being reinforced by a further 2,500 men from Drogheda, began to close in on the enemy. Realizing that Jones had left only token force to defend Dublin, Preston took a gamble and abandoned his siege lines intending to make a surprise thrust at the capital. Correctly gauging Preston's intentions, Jones set off in pursuit, bringing the Irishman to bay at Dungan's Hill, a mere 16km south of Trim on 8 August.

Cavalryman's buff coat and gauntlets, English c.1630. Part of the standard equipment for troopers of horse, the 'buff coat' made from tanned cowhide provided lightweight and flexible protection from sword cuts and possibly long-range musket or pistol fire. Sometimes worn alone, it was more often combined with the wearing of metal armour. (Courtesy of the Trustees, Royal Armouries, Leeds)

Jones's extensive experience as a cavalry officer notwithstanding, the battle was decided by Preston's relative inexperience in open warfare. Despite their superior numbers, the Confederate foot were deployed defensively in a large enclosed field, which prevented them from supporting the advance of the Irish horse who, outmanoeuvred by their enemy counterparts, were caught in a defile and cut to pieces. With their mounted supports in flight, the infantry's fate was sealed, the only question now being how many men could the Confederates bring safely off the field before the army disintegrated. Rallying the troops about him, Preston managed to force his way through a weak spot in the enemy lines with about half of his army, possibly about 3,000 men, before the Parliamentarian discipline was reasserted and the jaws of the steel trap closed on the remaining Irish troops.

Despite this signal victory, with the countryside devastated by the constant movement of bodies of armed men, Jones was in no position to capitalize on his success and returned to Dublin having, for the time being at least, neutralized the enemy threat to the Irish capital.

## CHANGES IN FORTUNE

Although crucial to the Confederates in terms of the loss of men and equipment, the defeat at Dungan's Hill and the subsequent battle of Knocknanuss in November 1647, where the Confederates' Munster Army under Taafe had been routed by Parliamentarian forces under Inchiquin, were not critical to their cause. Given the political tensions arising from the massacres of 1641, the options of the Kilkenny Assembly were strictly limited and thus, rather than any attempt being made to negotiate with Parliament, the main effect of the twin defeats was a steady marginalization in the position of the Papal nuncio, Rinuccini, and with this erosion came a renewed wooing of the leading Royalist supporters such as Ulick Burke, Marquess of Clanricarde.

As negotiations continued it became clear that, despite fundamental differences in their policies and their ultimate aims, both parties were realistic enough to acknowledge the fact that Parliament would need to be defeated before any lasting decision about Ireland's future could be implemented. Accordingly meetings took place in Paris, and a plan was developed whereby, in return for increased religious toleration – and tacit military assistance from France – Ormond would return to Ireland and assume overall direction of the war effort.

By the time of Ormond's return to Ireland in October 1648 the Confederates, realizing that he held the key to any future improvement in the position of Irish Catholics, became more reasonable in their aims and so a new treaty, 'The Second Ormond Peace', was signed on 17 January 1649. Under its provisions Ormond granted Catholics a limited form of religious freedom which was to be reviewed at a later date by a new, Royalist parliament. Militarily, the combined forces were to be reorganized with Ormond becoming Lord General, with Inchiquin and the Earl of Castlehaven as his lieutenant-generals of horse, and Sir Patrick Purcell as major-general of foot.

Politically marginalized, Rinuccini, the Papal nuncio, left Ireland in February but any hopes of Ó Neíll immediately lending his support to the alliance were dashed as the Ulsterman preferred to enter into private treaties with the Parliamentarian commanders whilst continuing with his wasting of Leinster. As a result, precious time was wasted in attempting to contain the maverick commander before Ormond could begin to mass his forces for the anticipated offensive against Dublin and the Parliamentarian garrisons in the Pale.

# DELIBERATIONS AT WESTMINSTER

Whilst Jones's victories over the Confederates had shown Parliament that whilst Dublin could be securely held for the Commonwealth, it was plain that in order to maintain the strategic initiative and prevent enclaves such as Derry and Drogheda from falling into enemy hands, additional forces would need to be sent to Ireland to defeat the enemy once and for all.

With Sir Thomas Fairfax – Parliament's most senior commander – unwilling to serve in Ireland, the search for a suitable replacement became increasingly more critical as news came of Ormond's return and the creation of the Royalist-Confederate coalition.

The members of the Council of State then settled on Lieutenant-General Oliver Cromwell, Fairfax's deputy, for the command of the new army – to be established with a field strength of 12,000 men – but instead of immediately accepting the new commission, their new commander kept the Council waiting a number of weeks, a time which he used to his own best advantage to secure a number of concessions which would grant him autonomy from political interference.

Accordingly, and during the time it took for the army to assemble, Cromwell began to make his plans and, anticipating that his forces would sail for Ireland sometime in late summer, entered into a correspondence with Jones in Dublin upon which would lie the foundations of his plan of campaign.

# CHRONOLOGY

## 1641

| | |
|---|---|
| 22 October | Outbreak of Irish Rising. |

## 1642

| | |
|---|---|
| 3 April | 2,500 Scots troops land at Carrickfergus. |
| July | Preston and Ó Neíll arrive in Ireland to join the rebel forces. |
| 24 October | Confederate Assembly holds inaugural meeting at Kilkenny. |

## 1643

| | |
|---|---|
| 15 September | Armistice signed between Ormond and the Confederates. |

## 1644

| | |
|---|---|
| 21 January | Ormond appointed Lord Lieutenant of Ireland. |
| 24 October | Parliament declares that 'quarter' will be denied to 'Irish' troops captured in either England or Wales. |

## 1645

| | |
|---|---|
| 20 December | Rinuccini arrives in Ireland as Papal nuncio. |

## 1646

| | |
|---|---|
| 5 June | Ó Neíll victorious over Monro's Scots at Benburb. |
| 30 July | 'First Ormond Peace' signed in Dublin but under pressure from Rinuccini, the Confederates disavow it almost immediately. |
| 14 November | Ormond enters into negotiations with Parliament for the handing over of Dublin in return for political and military guarantees. |

## 1647

| | |
|---|---|
| 19 June | Ormond formally surrenders possession of Dublin to Parliament. |
| 28 July | Ormond surrenders his office as Lord Lieutenant and leaves Ireland. |
| 8 August | Jones crushes Preston's Leinster forces at Dungan's Hill. |

## 1648

| | |
|---|---|
| 3 October | Ormond returns to Ireland to lead the Royalist-Confederate alliance. |

## 1649

| | |
|---|---|
| 17 January | 'Second Ormond Peace' signals the formation of the new alliance. |
| 29 January | Prince Rupert arrives at Kinsale with several Royalist warships. |
| 30 January | Execution of King Charles I. |
| 23 February | Rinuccini leaves Ireland. Ó Neíll refuses to accept the new treaty. |
| 8 May | Ó Neíll and Monck sign a three-month ceasefire. |
| 1 June | Ormond musters the Coalition forces at Clogrennan prior to marching on Dublin, which is reached on 19 June. |
| 22 June | Cromwell accepts Parliament's nomination as Lord General of Ireland. |
| 11 July | Inchiquin captures Drogheda. |
| 24 July | Inchiquin captures Dundalk. |
| 2 August | Jones defeats Ormond at Rathmines. |
| 15 August | Main body of Cromwell's Army lands at Ringsend, near Dublin. |
| 11 September | Cromwell takes Drogheda by storm. |

| | |
|---|---|
| 12 September | Venables detached with three regiments to stabilize the position in Ulster. |
| 11 October | Cromwell takes Wexford by storm. |
| 20 October | Ó Neíll agrees to join the Coalition forces. |
| 6 November | Death of Ó Neíll. |
| 2 December | Cromwell abandons siege of Waterford and goes into winter quarters. |

## 1650

| | |
|---|---|
| 29 January | Cromwell reorganizes his forces to move against Kilkenny. |
| 27 March | Surrender of Kilkenny. |
| 31 March | Broghill defeats Inchiquin at Mallow. |
| 26 April | Treaty of Cashel signed between Cromwell and a number of disaffected Protestant Royalists, thus isolating Ormond and his supporters. |
| 27 April | Cromwell arrives before Clonmel and summons the town to surrender. |
| 17 May | Parliamentarian assaults on Clonmel are repulsed with heavy loss. |
| 18 May | Clonmel surrenders to Cromwell 'under terms'. |
| 27 May | Cromwell leaves Ireland to assume command of operations against the Scots. He is succeeded by his son-in-law, Henry Ireton. |

# OPPOSING COMMANDERS

## PARLIAMENTARIAN

**Oliver Cromwell** (1599–1658). At the outbreak of the first Civil War and despite having no real experience of warfare, Cromwell proceeded to raise a troop of horse for service in the Parliamentarian forces. Mustered into the army of the Earl of Essex, he soon displayed not only an innate ability for tactical command but just as importantly, a firm grasp of logistics, traits which would make units under his command – at whatever level – that much more effective.

Cromwell's steady rise to prominence can be said too have begun with his victory at Gainsborough in July 1643, at which time he was given a colonelcy in the newly constituted Army of the Eastern Association, eventually being promoted to lieutenant-general of horse. At Marston Moor in July 1644, his methods of recruitment and training paid off when his by-now-veteran troopers made a major contribution to this crucial victory.

Exempted from having to resign his commission under the terms of the 'Self Denying Ordinance', which obliged 'political' officers to choose sitting in Parliament or serving in the army, Cromwell transferred to the embryonic 'New Model' Army and at Naseby in July 1645, it was again 'Old Noll's' horsemen that decided a hard-fought battle in favour of Parliament.

As the first Civil War drew to a close, Cromwell was hopeful of finding a method whereby the king could be returned to his throne at the head of a 'Parliamentary' government, but the monarch's continued duplicity and negotiations with the Scots meant that no such resolution was possible.

By now firmly convinced that Charles could no longer be trusted, and believing that it was both an act of justice and – perhaps more importantly – the will of God, Cromwell supported the process that resulted in the king's trial and was one of the signatories to his subsequent writ of execution.

Oliver Cromwell. One of Parliament's more successful generals, Cromwell's later reputation has been tarnished in modern years by the conduct of the troops under his command. (Courtesy of Bettmann-Corbis)

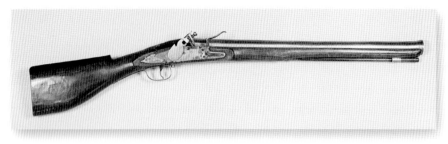

When in April 1649 Fairfax declined the command of the Irish expedition Cromwell, by now regarded as one of the finest soldiers in the country, was perhaps the most logical alternative choice. Widely respected for his devout nature, he stated that he would defer any decision whilst he sought spiritual guidance. Sceptics may suggest that this was a political move intended to outmanoeuvre the commissioners as, when he subsequently announced that he had received divine sanction, his acceptance of the expedition's command was subject to a number of non-negotiable conditions, such as dedicated naval support, the re-equipment of the army and a significant 'war chest' to cover the army's initial expenses.

Although marred by the question of his culpability in the massacres at Drogheda and Wexford, Cromwell's short campaign in Ireland is a model of tactical skill. On a number of occasions he demonstrated his superior ability in comparison with the enemy, the prime example being his limited strike into western Munster at the head of a flying column before turning about to rejoin the other elements of the army, which was at that stage converging on Kilkenny.

**Michael Jones** (d. 1649). Enlisting in the Government forces sent to Dublin in response to the Irish Rebellion of October 1641, Jones soon received a promotion as captain in a regiment of horse and, unable or unwilling to accept Ormond's ceasefire with the Catholic Confederates, he transferred his allegiance to Parliament, eventually rising to the rank of colonel and commanding the Parliamentarian forces at the siege of Chester in September 1645.

When Ormond made his overtures to Parliament early in 1647, Jones was clearly the best choice to assume the military governorship of Dublin – he had grown up in Ireland, had served under Ormond and was showing himself to be an exceptional battlefield commander.

Having secured the Irish capital, Jones successfully moved to break the Confederate siege of Trim and, on his return journey, was engaged by their Leinster Army at Dungan's Hill where he shattered arguably the best trained and best equipped of the Confederate armies, a defeat that indirectly served to push the Confederates towards a rapprochement with Ormond. With the destruction of the Leinster Army, Jones informed Parliament that he was now in a position to take the offensive and reconquer Ireland but a combination of bad weather, disease and an aggressive campaign by Éoghan 'Rua' Ó Neíll forced him back on the defensive.

Backsword, 'mortuary' style, English *c.*1640. Deriving its name from the hilt design, this particular example is reputed to have been carried by Cromwell during his Irish campaign. (Courtesy the Trustees, Royal Armouries, Leeds)

This was the status quo that would last for almost two years until June 1649 when Ormond led the Royalist-Confederate forces against Dublin. Heavily outnumbered, but with the welcome reinforcement of almost 2,000 veteran troops which formed the advance guard of Cromwell's Army, he sallied out of the city and engaged Ormond's forces at Rathmines on 2 August, attacking the enemy as they advanced piecemeal. Using his limited number of cavalrymen to great effect Jones shattered the Coalition forces, removing the threat to the capital in what could be argued as being the most crucial engagement of the war as, without a secure port, Cromwell's forces would have been unable to land.

As a reward for his earlier services, Jones was promoted to lieutenant-general and served Cromwell ably, first by leading the advance guard in the Drogheda campaign and then at the siege of Wexford where he commanded the detached force which captured Rosslare Fort. As the weather worsened and the troops withdrew from the unsuccessful siege of Waterford, Jones like Cromwell and a great many of the army fell sick, succumbing to fever on 10 December having shown, if only for a short time, that he was one of Cromwell's most capable subordinates.

**Henry Ireton** (1611–51), A lawyer by profession, Ireton spent the early period of the Civil War as a simple officer of Parliamentarian horse, but following Cromwell's victory at Gainsborough in July 1643 he began an association with his commanding officer that would eventually see him rise to become Commissary-General of the Eastern Association, in which capacity he saw action at Marston Moor, Second Newbury and Naseby, as well as a number of lesser actions. In June 1646 he further cemented this close relationship by marrying Cromwell's eldest daughter, Bridget.

At the fall of Colchester in 1648, during the suppression of a Royalist-inspired rising in Kent and Essex, Ireton was reputedly responsible for drafting the orders to execute the captured enemy commanders on the grounds that they had allegedly broken their previously given parole that they would no longer bear arms against Parliament. Later in the year, he was instrumental in drafting the *Army Remonstrance* that uncompromisingly placed the responsibility for the conflict firmly at the feet of the Crown, effectively setting in motion the chain of events that would lead to the trial and execution of King Charles.

Whilst plans were being made for the expedition to Ireland, and a second in command whom he could trust, Cromwell requested that Ireton be appointed his deputy with a requisite promotion to major-general. Although the petition was granted, Michael Jones effectively assumed this role from his promotion to lieutenant-general in August 1649 until his death in December of that year. Following the failure to take Waterford in November and, with both Cromwell and Jones falling critically ill, Ireton took command of the army, leading it into winter quarters.

Following Cromwell's recall to England in May 1650 to prepare for the Scottish campaign, Ireton assumed command of the Parliamentarian forces, a position that he held until his death in 1651 following his capture of Limerick.

# ROYALIST

**James Butler, 12th Earl of Ormond** (1610–88). Unlike the vast majority of his extended family, Ormond was raised as a Protestant, and as a result was a key figure in the Irish administration, serving under Strafford during his tenure as Lord Deputy of Ireland. When the Irish rose in rebellion against the Crown, Ormond found himself in command of the Government forces around Dublin and, although without real military experience, he led the army to victory at Kilrush over rebel forces commanded by his cousin, Richard Butler, Viscount Mountgarret.

Capitalizing on this initial success by clearing the outskirts of Dublin of enemy forces, he created a cordon sanitaire around the city, but a number of his political opponents combined to have his commission revoked on the grounds of his familial relationships with many of the senior enemy commanders. Ormond's fall from grace was, however, only a temporary one and, during the autumn of 1642, at the beginning of the English Civil War, he returned with a royal warrant, once again giving him control of His Majesty's Forces in Ireland.

Backsword, 'mortuary' style, English c.1640. Hilt detail of the weapon attributed to Oliver Cromwell. (Courtesy the Trustees, Royal Armouries, Leeds)

Despite this seemingly imposing commission, Ormond's position was hamstrung from the start, as the outbreak of hostilities between king and Parliament effectively meant that there would be no prospect of future reinforcement; indeed the reality was rather that that the Crown viewed the army in Ireland as a reservoir from which additional troops could be drawn for the conflict in England.

Constantly under pressure from the king to withdraw troops from Ireland, Ormond signed a ceasefire agreement with the Confederates in September 1643, under the terms of which, in return for the surrender of territory to the Confederates, they would also undertake to support a fixed number of troops to fight for the Crown. The treaty was a bitter pill for many of his supporters and a number transferred their allegiance to Parliament, thereby undermining his position even further.

In 1646 Ormond attempted to renegotiate a treaty with the Confederates, but in this he was thwarted by the influence of the controversial Papal nuncio, Rinuccini, and with his position being steadily eroded he entered into an agreement whereby in return for the transfer of Dublin, Parliamentarian forces would protect the interests of Royalist sympathizers remaining in areas not controlled by the Confederates.

In August 1647, he left Ireland to go into voluntary exile, whilst a Parliamentarian army under Michael Jones finally secured the Dublin Pale for Parliament, defeating the Confederates at the battle of Dungan's Hill.

Ormond's exile was relatively short as, following a string of defeats at Jones's hands the Confederates became more amenable to a compromise with the Crown and a new treaty was signed in January 1649. He took command of the Coalition forces but was heavily defeated by Jones in an uncoordinated battle at Rathmines on 2 August.

After the battle Ormond adopted a new strategy, attempting to wear down Cromwell's Army by forcing it to prosecute a number of expensive sieges but with the loss of the cream of his army at Drogheda, his remaining

forces proved to be no real match for the enemy. Despite continued losses, Ormond remained in command but was unable to resolve the distrust that permeated the two allied camps and the bulk of his Protestant forces offered their allegiance to Parliament in May 1650, a defection that led to his removal as commander-in-chief and his going into a second, enforced period of exile which would last until the Restoration in 1660.

**Murrough O'Brien, 6th Baron Inchiquin** (1614–74). Like many of his contemporaries, Inchiquin had learned his trade on the battlefields of Europe during the Thirty Years War, having fought for three years with the Spanish Army of Italy (1636–39). Although a Gaelic chieftain, Inchiquin was nonetheless a Protestant and with the outbreak of the Irish Rebellion of October 1641, he accordingly sided with the Government, serving with the Munster forces commanded by his father-in-law, Sir William St Leger, until the latter's death in July 1642.

Quickly assuming command of the army, Inchiquin led it to victory over the Confederates at Liscarroll on 2 September, a victory that consolidated governmental control of the south-west until the negotiation of the armistice.

Snubbed by King Charles I over the Presidency of Munster, Inchiquin declared his support for Parliament and turning on his former allies, established his control over Munster with a brutal campaign culminating in September 1647 with the sack of the Rock of Cashel and, two months later, with his victory over Taaffe at Knocknanuss.

The unlikely rapprochement came to a sudden end on 11 February 1648 when Parliament passed the 'Vote of No Addresses'. Effectively a vote of no confidence in King Charles I and a censure of his entire reign, it was a declaration that Parliament would implement a new system of government without reference to the monarchy. Shocked by the implications of such a move, Inchiquin changed sides once more, becoming one of Ormond's leading subordinates following the 'Second Ormond Peace' of September 1648, which effectively patched up an anti-Parliamentarian coalition between Royalist and Confederate forces.

During the 1649 campaigning season, Inchiquin was firstly tasked with ejecting the dissident Éoghan 'Rua' Ó Néill from Leinster and, as Ormond opened his campaign to take Dublin, Inchiquin was sent north with a substantial force to capture Trim, Drogheda and Dundalk, effectively driving a wedge between the Parliamentarian garrisons around Dublin and in Ulster. With mounting anticipation of a landing by Parliamentarian forces under Cromwell, he was sent by Ormond to assume command in Munster and defend the south-west, and so was absent from the crucial battle of Rathmines, where his experience would have been invaluable.

In October 1649, Inchiquin's position worsened with the landing of a Parliamentarian force under the command of Roger Boyle, 1st Baron Broghill, and colonels Phayre and Stubber, eventually leading to the defection of a number of his garrisons to Parliament. Over the course of the winter he reorganized his forces, but in March 1650 was brought to battle and heavily defeated by Broghill at Mallow after which he was obliged to retreat northwards into Connacht.

Seeing that there was no hope of victory against Cromwell's forces, Inchiquin chose to go into exile in France where he was created 1st Earl Inchiquin by King Charles II, eventually adopting the Catholic faith before returning to Ireland during the Restoration of 1660. Ironically, he was subsequently considered for the position of Lord President of Munster by the new regime, but was again passed over, this time on account of his Catholicism.

**Sir Arthur Aston** (1590–1649). The younger son of a Catholic landowning family, Aston began his military career in 1613 in Russian service during the Polish–Muscovite War (1605–18). When peace was signed between the belligerents, he returned briefly to England before enlisting in the Polish Army, at that time engaged against the Ottoman Empire.

Following the outbreak of the Thirty Years War, Aston fought for Poland against the Swedes after their invasion of Livonia in 1621, and following the cessation of hostilities a decade later the newly promoted Lieutenant-Colonel Aston returned to England where he raised a regiment of troops, this time for service in the Swedish Army.

Aston fought in the fateful Lützen campaign of 1632, remaining in Swedish service until 1640 when he accepted a commission as sergeant major-general of Viscount Conway's English Army for the invasion of Scotland. Following the defeat at Newburn he was given a brigade by Strafford, the new army commander, and on 17 September was appointed sergeant major-general of the Yorkshire Trained Bands.

Knighted in 1641, Aston offered his services to the Crown when relations between king and Parliament deteriorated into open warfare but was refused a commission on account of his religion. By the battle of Edgehill on 23 October 1642, however, his petition had been accepted and he was appointed colonel-general of Dragoons.

Before the end of the year, he had been appointed governor of the strategically important town of Reading and almost immediately began to alienate the populace as he strove to improve the town's defences. In April 1643, Parliamentarian forces under the Earl of Essex besieged Reading. However, after repulsing several enemy attacks Aston was rendered *hors de combat* when struck on the head by falling brickwork, and whilst he was thus incapacitated, the town surrendered. Amongst his numerous enemies rumours were circulated that the injury was feigned, and it is certain that memory of the loss of Reading contributed to Aston's actions prior to the siege of Drogheda in September 1649.

**BOTTOM**
Reconstruction of a Confederate infantry colour. Combining the red cross of St Patrick in a white or yellow cantonal field, Confederate infantry colours often displayed a religious theme. Here we see the Virgin Mary holding an infant Jesus, whilst crushing Satan in the form of a snake. To signify loyalty to the king, the colour also bears a crown imperial with the royal cipher 'CR' and the Latin phrase *Vivat Carolus Rex* – long live King Charles. (Courtesy of Seán Ó Brógáin/Cavan Museum)

Sir Phelim Ó Neíll (1603–53). Initially leader of the Ulster Confederates, Ó Neíll was overshadowed by his more famous cousin, Éoghan 'Rua', but his masterful defence of Charlemont in 1650 led to one of the few occasions of a Confederate garrison being granted full honours of war. Captured in February 1653, he was taken to Dublin and executed for treason. (Courtesy of the National Gallery of Ireland. Photo © National Gallery of Ireland)

Whatever the truth behind the accusations, Aston's career did not suffer, and, after service as major-general to Prince Rupert, he was appointed governor of Oxford, a position that he held until incapacitated by a riding accident in which he lost his leg. Following the 'Second Ormond Peace' and on Prince Rupert's recommendation, Aston became one of Ormond's military advisers. Following the conclusion of a council of war on 23 August 1649 and in view of his extensive experience, he was fatefully appointed military governor of Drogheda.

# CONFEDERATE

**Hugh 'Dubh' Ó Neíll** (1611–60). Having served for several years in the Spanish Army of Flanders, Hugh 'Dubh' was amongst the party of 300 Irish officers who returned to Ireland in July 1642 with his uncle, Éoghan 'Rua' Ó Neíll, to form the veteran core of an Ulster Confederate Army. Taken prisoner during an ambush by Scots Covenanter forces, Ó Neíll remained a captive until the aftermath of the battle of Benburb on 5 June 1646, as a result of which he was released and rejoined his uncle's forces, taking part in the desultory campaign in Ulster and Leinster.

In late 1649, Ó Neíll was sent south with 2,000 Ulster veterans to garrison the strategic town of Clonmel, which was eventually besieged by Cromwell in May 1650. Proving adept at defensive warfare, he managed not only to inflict severe casualties upon the Parliamentarian forces, but also used the opportunity afforded by surrender negotiations – between Cromwell and the civil authorities – to withdraw his troops from the town under cover of darkness, eventually rejoining the garrison of Limerick, of which he later assumed command. Shortly after the siege of Clonmel, Cromwell left for England having suffered his only defeat of the campaign.

An initial attempt in October 1650, by Parliamentarian forces under the command of Henry Ireton, was a failure and it wasn't until the following summer before a second attempt was made. Having learnt from Clonmel, Ireton's tactics were simply to blockade the city and starve the defenders into submission. Aided by dissent within the defenders' ranks, and an outbreak of disease that badly affected both sides, the matter was resolved when the Parliamentarian heavy artillery breached the city walls, leaving Ó Neíll no option other than surrender or face a mutiny by elements of the garrison.

Exempted from the terms of capitulation and sentenced to execution, Ó Neíll was taken to London where the Spanish ambassador secured his release on the grounds that he was a subject of the king of Spain. Under the proviso that he would never serve in action against Parliament, Ó Neíll returned to Spain where he was promoted to general of artillery. Remaining in the Spanish service, Ó Neíll died of disease in 1660, following an unsuccessful attempt to secure his recognition as 5th Earl of Tyrone.

# OPPOSING FORCES

## PARLIAMENTARIAN FORCES

Once its members had been convinced of the necessity of mounting a military expedition to Ireland, Parliament had to make two crucial decisions – how many men were to be sent and, more importantly, who was to command them. Initially, Sir Thomas Fairfax had been proposed as commanding general, but as that worthy had declined the offer, it was suggested that the position be offered to his subordinate, Oliver Cromwell. As careful in the corridors of power as he was on the battlefield, Cromwell refused to commit himself, limiting his response to an endorsement of the decision to mount the expedition: 'I had rather be overrun with a Cavalierish interest [than] of a Scotch interest; I had rather be overrun with a Scotch interest than an Irish interest; and I think of all, this is the most dangerous.'

Should he accept the command, he continued, his position would need to combine both civil and military power and just as important the conditions under which the army was mustered would need to be attractive in order to prevent desertion and defections, and above all it would need to be well equipped and well supplied.

Having come to terms with his conscience, Cromwell formally accepted command of the Irish expedition on 30 March, fully satisfied that the forces coming under his command would be politically and, above all, religiously reliable. Their antipathy for the Catholic church notwithstanding, many of the officers and men were now tending to view the coming campaign under purely religious terms, with lurid reports of the massacre of large numbers of unarmed Protestants leading many to regard the expedition as a crusade against Catholicism and the Irish.

On 20 April the units destined to serve in Ireland were selected by lot – a child drawing a slip of paper from a hat, for each unit, and then presenting it to the senior regimental officer present. Blank slips meant that the unit would remain in England, whilst those that were marked 'Ireland' were appointed to the expeditionary force. In all four regiments of horse – commanded by Henry Ireton, Adrian Scrope, John Lambert and Thomas Horton – and four of foot – those of Isaac Ewer, Richard Deane, George Cooke and John Hewson – were chosen

VIVAT
CAROLVS
REX

CR

EXVRGAT:DEVS:DISSIPEXTVR:INIMICI

Confederate infantry colour c.1649. Again we have the common religious theme, this time the risen Christ, interestingly enough carrying a standard with the cross of St George, England's national device. Underneath the cantonal cross of St Patrick is the royal monogram and crown imperial with the Latin inscription *Vivat Carolus Rex*. (Courtesy Seán Ó Brógáin)

in this manner to augment the units already being recruited to full strength prior to embarkation, namely John Reynolds' regiment of horse and the foot regiments of Hercules Huncks and Robert Venables. To round off the main body of the expeditionary force, a similar draw was made within Okey's regiment of dragoons and five companies under the leadership of Major Daniel Abbott were chosen by lot for service in Ireland. The unit commanders were enjoined to recruit their regiments up to full strength and proceed to Milford Haven in South Wales, Cromwell's chosen port of embarkation.

Eventually the forces under Cromwell's command were to comprise some four regiments of horse, five companies of dragoons and six regiments of foot, totalling 4,000 and 8,000 men respectively to which was added a train of approximately 60 cannon including a number of heavy pieces intended to reduce enemy fortifications.

Despite the manner in which it was conducted the selection was, however, not infallible and a number of changes were almost immediately necessary. With John Lambert currently in the north of England observing the Scots, it was decided that his regiment of horse could not be spared for Ireland and would need to be replaced, whilst some days after the draw had been made elements of Ireton's and Scrope's regiments mutinied against the service and had to be suppressed by troops under the joint command of Fairfax and Cromwell. For the regiments of foot, although the movement to the embarkation ports was not without incident, the only major change was necessitated by the appointment of Richard Deane to a naval command as one of the three 'generals-at-sea', which temporarily left his regiment without a commanding officer.

These disruptions to the expedition's order of battle were simply resolved by firstly appointing Cromwell to the vacant colonelcy of Deane's regiment of foot, whilst simultaneously raising a double-strength regiment of horse, again with Cromwell as colonel, which would operate tactically two regimental-sized 'divisions' under the command of lieutenant-colonels Jerome Sankey and Thomas Shelbourne

Although the composition of Cromwell's Army had been established, the question of finance still needed to be addressed and indeed threatened to defeat the expeditionary force before it met the enemy in battle. Firstly, funds had to be secured to resolve the soldiers' arrears in pay, and then sufficient set aside to meet not only future payments, but also to meet the cost of procuring the supplies needed to maintain the troops in the field. Secondly, and of equal importance, was the need to support the beleaguered garrisons in Ireland who were even then coming under increasing pressure from Ormond's forces. The problem was that the Commonwealth Government was almost bankrupt, with military spending spiralling out of control, and no one was prepared to advance them the funds to equip and supply Cromwell's forces whilst the Government debt remained outstanding.

Legislation was subsequently passed that allowed Parliament to dispose of church lands, the sale of which realized a little over £1 million, which was cynically followed by an increase in the property tax intended to bring in a similar amount. With the national debt somewhat resolved, the Government was able to obtain funding from the City of London, which not only provided Cromwell's 'war chest' of £100,000 in cash, but also generated enough credit so that the regiments could be at least given a new issue of clothing. The sums raised, however, were not sufficient to clear the soldiers' pay arrears and there were some signs of discontent amongst the marching columns. It was not until July, when property of the exiled royal family was put up for sale, that the deficit was cleared and the Government given enough breathing space to implement a new tax regime that would raise sufficient revenues to meet the ever-increasing military expenditure.

## ROYALIST FORCES

On his return to Ireland in October 1648, the situation facing Ormond was discouraging in the extreme. Instead of an organized body, opposition to the Commonwealth had degenerated into a loose grouping of mutually antagonistic factions that would need to be welded into a viable coalition if the enemy were to be defeated. It is therefore a testament to his political skill that, despite these divisions he was able to bring many of the disparate factions together. In this very success, however, lay the ultimate seeds of his failure for whilst an able politician, Ormond was not a soldier and thus the majority of his decisions were made with a political bias rather than a military one.

Reconstruction of a Confederate junior officer c.1649. There is little difference between the illustration of the Confederate pikeman on page 85 and this reconstruction of a junior officer – the sole distinguishing features being the wearing of a broadsword rather than a *sgian* and the fact that this officer is wearing a comb morion of an earlier period. (Courtesy Seán Ó Brógáin)

By reconciling the needs of the Crown with those of the Confederates and, to a lesser degree, the Ulster Scots, Ormond was now able to gather together an army that, excluding garrisons, could put over 20,000 men into the field. It was a force that dwarfed that available to Jones at the beginning of the Rathmines campaign (c.3,200 men) and would still give Ormond the numerical advantage even after the landing of Cromwell's expeditionary force.

However, there were considerable problems with the Royalist forces. With no dedicated manufacturing base, as was available in England, arms and munitions had to be imported into the country and, as the major ports began to fall into enemy hands, the supply of armaments became that much more critical, especially after the disaster at Rathmines and the loss of Drogheda.

# ORDERS OF BATTLE

**PARLIAMENTARIAN FORCES, AUGUST 1649**

Garrison of Dublin – Colonel Michael Jones (later lieutenant-general of horse)
Regiments of horse

> Michael Jones
>
> Chidley Coote
>
> John Ponsonby
>
> John Reynolds (ex-Cromwell)

Regiments of foot

> Sir John Borlase
>
> James Castle
>
> Roger Fenwick
>
> Hercules Huncks (ex-Cromwell)
>
> Anthony Hungerford
>
> John Kynaston
>
> Thomas Long
>
> John Moore
>
> Owen O'Connolly
>
> Robert Tothill
>
> Robert Venables (ex-Cromwell)

Garrison of Derry – Sir Charles Coote
Regiments of horse

> Sir Charles Coote

Regiments of foot

> Sir Charles Coote

The Army for Ireland – Lord General Oliver Cromwell
Regiments of horse

> Henry Ireton
>
> Thomas Horton
>
> Jerome Sankey
>
> Thomas Shelbourne

Regiments of foot

> Oliver Cromwell
>
> George Cooke
>
> Isaac Ewer
>
> John Hewson

Detachment of five companies of dragoons commanded by Major Daniel Abbott

For service in Munster under Baron Broghill
Regiments of foot

> Robert Phayre
>
> Peter Stubber

ROYALIST FORCES

Garrison of Drogheda –Sir Arthur Aston (September 1649)

Troops of horse

Sir James Preston (41)

Sir John Dongan (30)

Lieutenant-Colonel Dungan (29)

Major Butler (36)

Captain Harpole (29)

Captain Plunkett (29)

Captain Fleming (69)

Captain Finglas (57)

Regiments of foot

Lord Lieutenant (539)

Colonel Byrne (480)

Colonel Wall (485)

Colonel Warren (537)

Sir Henry Titchbourne*

Lt-Col Griffin Kavenagh (c.500)

*Formerly part of the Commonwealth garrison of Drogheda.*

Garrison of Waterford – Lieutenant-General Richard Farrell (November 1649)

Troops of horse

Capt Walter Dalton (32)

Capt Lewis Farrell (35)

Regiments of foot

Lieutenant-General Farrell (434)

Colonel Turlough McArt Oge O'Neill (230)

Garrison of Clonmel – Major-General Hugh 'Dubh' Ó Neíll (April 1650)

Troops of horse

Lieutenant-Colonel Fennell (19)

Captain Pierce Butler (42)

Regiments of foot

Colonel Turlough O'Neill (440)

Colonel Philip McHugh O'Reilly (1,006)

Colonel Edmund FitzMaurice* (52)

*Formerly part of the Royalist garrison of Cashel.*

# OPPOSING PLANS

## PARLIAMENTARIAN PLANS

Aware that time was of crucial importance – his campaign would last only as long as Parliament could continue to finance the troops in the field – Cromwell's intended plan of operations was to comprise three elements. Firstly he planned to relieve Jones in Dublin and, having consolidated the position there, open up lines of communication with the Commonwealth enclaves in Ulster and Munster, thereby establishing a single command structure to coordinate field operations. Next, he was determined to induce Ormond to give battle and, having met the enemy's main field army, defeat it and thereby seize the tactical as well as strategic initiative. Finally, and with the other preconditions having been met, his intention was systematically to reduce the Coalition's principal strongholds one after the other until such time that they conceded defeat.

Given that it was the least mobile component of the army, and that he intended to take the field with the least possible delay, on 3 July Cromwell sent his artillery train by sea to Dublin in advance of the rest of the expedition, reasoning that it would take longer to ship the cannon and prepare them for action than it would to ready the remainder of the army for operations in the field. Then, when it became apparent that Ormond was advancing upon Dublin, threatening his intended landing site of Ringsend, he decided to move a number of regiments immediately – namely those of Reynolds, Huncks and Venables – and transfer them to Dublin in order to reinforce the garrison there.

The news of Jones' crushing victory at Rathmines on 2 August effectively accelerated the realization of Cromwell's campaign objectives by removing Ormond's field army from the equation, compelling him to re-evaluate his plans and move his headquarters immediately to Dublin in order to confer with his newly promoted lieutenant-general of horse. As the expedition had still

Flintlock holster pistol of military type, English *c.*1640. For use at close quarters, the flintlock holster pistol represented developing technology, although – like the infantry musket – its weight could also see it employed as a makeshift club in close combat. (Courtesy of the Trustees, Royal Armouries, Leeds)

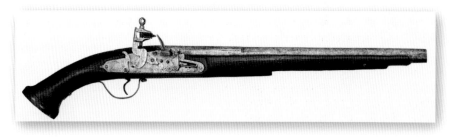

not formed, and leaving Ireton in charge at Milford Haven, he embarked his cavalry regiment into 36 ships, and set sail for Dublin on 13 August.

Two days later, the rest of the expeditionary force – with the exception of Horton's regiment, which was still forming and would sail alone later – boarded their transports, but instead of sailing directly to link up with the forces in Dublin, the flotilla sailed first for the Munster coast. This diversion has given rise to many theories about Cromwell's intentions, with a number of commentators such as Abbott, Gardiner and more recently Ian Gentles and James Scott Wheeler, referring to a plan by which Cromwell intended to divide his army and attack the enemy on two fronts.

The truth is that two units (Phayre's and Stubber's) had been earmarked for service in Munster from the outset and, in an effort to secure suitable landing facilities, Cromwell had spent much time and effort in attempting to suborn a number of enemy officers in the hope that one, or more, could be bribed to turn their coats against Ormond and allow the Parliamentarian forces to land unopposed. In the event, none of the local commanders acceded to Cromwell's coercion and, unable to land, the regiments in question were obliged to continue to Dublin with the rest of Ireton's command.

A week after Cromwell's landing in Ireland, the final element of the expeditionary force, Horton's regiment of horse, set sail from Milford Haven. Arriving too late to take part in the siege and capture of Drogheda, the troops would remain in Dublin until the successful conclusion of the initial phase of Cromwell's plan.

Burgonet-style cavalryman's helmet. One of the more common types of cavalry helmet, this example has an articulated neck guard for protection and ease of movement and a fixed visor to protect the face. (Courtesy of the Trustees, Royal Armouries, Leeds)

# ROYALIST PLANS

Advised by his agents of the preparations for the Parliamentarian expeditionary force, and despite the fact that he was more of a courtier than a soldier, Ormond was also realist enough to know where the direction of the Royalist war effort should lie – the recapture of Dublin and the vital harbour facilities at Ringsend. With Commonwealth forces in Ulster being contained by Coalition troops, and with the southern province of Munster in safe hands, there were two ways in which this could be achieved, and so, ever the politician, he made overtures to Jones in an attempt to suborn the Parliamentarian officer and induce him to join the Royalist coalition. Interestingly enough he declined to appeal to any loyalty Jones might have to an exiled, albeit Protestant monarch, instead concentrating on what he saw as the duplicity of the Council of State in London, and playing upon the outrage generated by the trial and execution of King Charles, writing '… now that the mask of hypocrisy (by which the Independent Army hath ensnared and enslaved all estates and degrees of men) is laid aside, now that barefaced they evidently appear … having laid violent and sacrilegious hands upon and murdered God's anointed and our king …' Jones's response was swift in coming and typically laconic, reaffirming his belief that the Westminster Parliament was the sole legally appointed governmental body in either England or Ireland and that, by virtue of his continued allegiance to the deposed house of Stuart, Ormond's own commission as lord lieutenant was invalid.

Accepting that a political solution – however unlikely – was now closed to him, Ormond began to marshal his forces for a thrust at the Irish capital. Despite his lack of military experience, he was confident that the superior numbers available to him would guarantee a successful conclusion to the campaign, and that by the time Cromwell's force was ready to sail, the inevitable Royalist capture of Dublin would have made the whole matter academic.

Despite the simplicity of Ormond's plan there was one crucial factor that would have a deciding effect upon its chances of success – quite simply, his major advantage lay in the number of cavalry that he could put into the field, and their presence was dependent upon the amount of available grazing for their horses. Accordingly, the troops were late in mustering, assembling at Clogrennan in Co. Carlow on 1 June.

With almost 15,000 men under arms and more under way, and despite the undercurrents of tension that almost perpetually simmered between Catholics and Protestants, there was a tangible confidence in the Royalist camp – it was known that Jones had less than 4,000 men in Dublin and also that the city's dilapidated defences were in such need of repair that they would be of little use in the face of a determined attack.

There were but two questions that needed to be answered: firstly, should Ormond move directly on Dublin and make an immediate assault, or should he instead blockade the city whilst operations against the outlying enemy garrisons were prosecuted and an armed wedge driven between the Commonwealth enclaves in Ulster and Leinster? The second, and possibly the most important question that required an answer was succinctly 'What were the intentions of Éoghan 'Rua' Ó Néill?'

Following the schism in the Confederate ranks, the Ulsterman had shown himself to be more than willing to come to an accommodation with his foes in order to pursue the infighting that had characterized much of the Assembly's existence to date and, having already done so much to preserve the cause of his enemies at the expense of his former allies he, like Jones, now had no inclination to accede to Ormond's invitation to find common cause against the Commonwealth, preferring instead to wait upon developments. In any event, Royalist successes in Ulster would serve to attract Ó Néill's attention and prevent him from interfering with Ormond's campaign.

Deciding to opt for the safest course of action, Ormond detached Inchiquin with 4,000 men to reduce Drogheda, Trim and Dundalk whilst he would lead the main body of the army on to Dublin and place the city under a loose blockade. He had hoped that Prince Rupert and his squadron at Kinsale would have been able to interdict the seaborne approaches to Dublin, but this small force was itself being blockaded in port by a superior Commonwealth squadron under Robert Blake. As the Royalists continued their advance Jones made a number of sallies out of the city, each time forcing Ormond's troops to deploy for battle, thereby trading space for time, time that was not only needed to repair Dublin's crumbling defences, but also to give any reinforcements the chance to arrive before the city was besieged.

Skirting the western suburbs of Dublin, Ormond continued northwards, eventually establishing a base at Finglas, and for some weeks both sides played a game of cat and mouse, launching raid and counter-raid, probing the enemy's lines whilst they built up their strength and consolidated their positions. It was not all one-sided however, and although Moore's welcome reinforcements arrived safely from England in mid-June, Inchiquin's successful completion of his mission on 24 July meant that he was now able

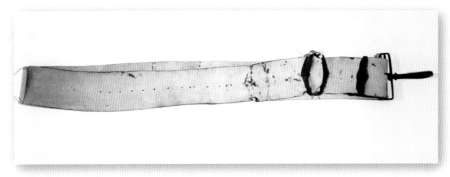

to move to rejoin Ormond, bringing with him not only his part of the army and the artillery train but also a number of valuable recruits in the form of the former garrisons of Drogheda and Dundalk, many of whom had since elected to defect to the Royalists as a way of securing food and clothing.

Even as the army reunited, vague reports were starting to come in from Munster coupling news of civil unrest with rumours of Parliamentarian landings. Accordingly, Inchiquin was sent to the south-west accompanied by his Lifeguard and two regiments of veteran horse with instructions to quell any discontent and reorganize the Royalist forces in the south.

It was the moment that Ormond had long been planning for. Against the odds he had somehow managed to unite the various partisan groups, Catholics, Protestants, English, Irish and Ulster-Scots, and forge from these disparate elements an army that now held every advantage over the enemy, an army that if resolutely led – and even in Inchiquin's absence there was still no shortage of experienced commanders within its ranks – would surely be able to take possession of Dublin and resolve the campaign at a single stroke. Yet, at the moment of decision, when he should possibly have adopted a bold course of action and ordered the attack, Ormond hesitated, his indecision allowing the initiative to slip away from him momentarily.

He needed to review his plan of campaign and carry it through to a favourable conclusion. Accordingly, the army was ordered to break camp early on the morning of 25 July and, leaving some 2,500 men under the command of Thomas, 4th Viscount Dillon, to cover the northern approaches to Dublin, Ormond moved southwards again, crossing the Liffey and marching toward the suburb of Rathmines.

# THE CAMPAIGN

## THE GREAT VICTORY, RATHMINES, 2 AUGUST 1649

In order to press the enemy as close as possible, Ormond decided to fortify the ruins of Baggotrath Castle, which lay between the site of his new camp at Rathmines and the walls of Dublin. On 1 August he gave orders for a party of 2,500 men under Sir Patrick Purcell to occupy the castle and place it in a state of defensive readiness. His intent was not only to create a linchpin upon which to base his forward lines and dominate the open terrain to the south of the city, but also to secure a suitable site from which his artillery could bombard the harbour at Ringsend and, in doing so, disrupt the movement of enemy shipping in the Liffey estuary. Setting out shortly after darkness fell, and despite the fact that Baggotrath was only a mile or so distant from the Royalist camp, Purcell and his men inexplicably failed to arrive before daybreak on the following morning, in full view of the enemy sentries patrolling Dublin's walls.

Increasingly aware of Baggotrath's isolated position, Ormond then decided to reinforce Purcell by sending him an additional 2,000 horse under the command of Sir William Vaughan, his fears being made more acute when, on arriving at the castle to discuss the situation with both officers he discovered that Purcell had merely contented himself with occupying the ruins and that little work had begun on improving the defences. Exhausted after a series of command meetings that had lasted most of the night, Ormond then returned to Rathmines and, giving orders that the army should stand to in readiness for anticipated enemy action he retired to his tent to sleep.

Armed with the clarity of hindsight and knowing full well of his opponent's reputation as an aggressive commander, this was the worst possible course of action for Ormond to have taken, for as soon as he was informed of the enemy's dispositions, Jones began to plan a limited counterattack aimed at dislodging Purcell's men from the castle and regaining control of the surrounding area.

As the early morning mist began to clear, Jones led a force of some 4,000 foot and 1,200 horse in the pastureland to the south of the city, the bulk of the troops coming from the veteran regiments of Reynolds, Huncks and Venables, recently arrived from England. The plan, such as it was, was simply for the column to engage the enemy as quickly as possible, the Parliamentarian horse engaging their opposite numbers whilst the infantry stormed the improvised defences. Despite the disparity in numbers, the

# The Rathmines campaign, June–August 1649

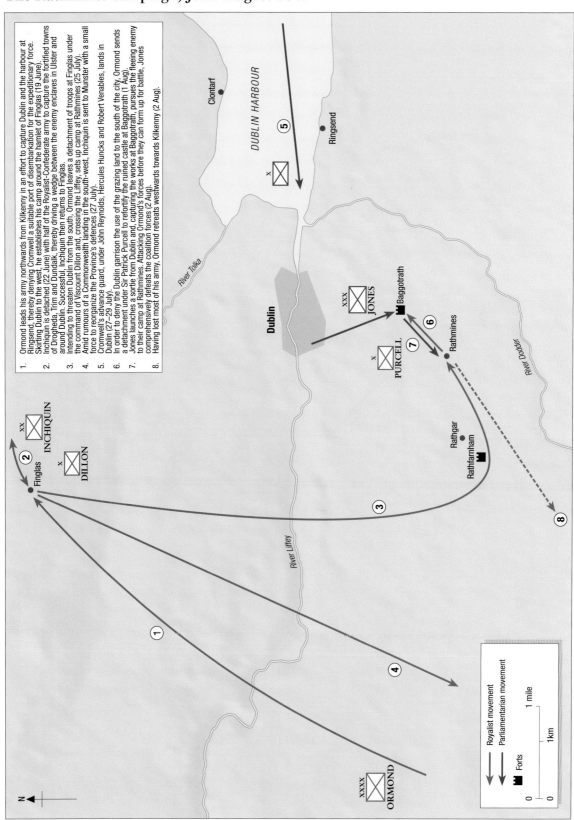

1. Ormond leads his army northwards from Kilkenny in an effort to capture Dublin and the harbour at Ringsend, thereby denying Cromwell a suitable port of disembarkation for the expeditionary force. Skirting Dublin to the west, he establishes his camp around the hamlet of Finglas (19 June).
2. Inchiquin is detached (22 June) with half of the Royalist-Confederate army to capture the fortified towns of Drogheda, Trim and Dundalk, thereby driving a wedge between the enemy enclaves in Ulster and around Dublin. Successful, Inchiquin then returns to Finglas.
3. Intending to threaten Dublin from the south, Ormond leaves a detachment of troops at Finglas under the command of Viscount Dillon and, crossing the Liffey, sets up camp at Rathmines (25 July).
4. Amid rumours of a Commonwealth landing in the south-west, Inchiquin is sent to Munster with a small force to reorganize the Province's defences (27 July).
5. Cromwell's advance guard, under John Reynolds, Hercules Huncks and Robert Venables, lands in Dublin (27–29 July).
6. In order to deny the Dublin garrison the use of the grazing land to the south of the city, Ormond sends a detachment under Sir Patrick Purcell to refortify the ruined castle at Baggotrath (1 Aug).
7. Jones launches a sortie from Dublin and, capturing the works at Baggotrath, pursues the fleeing enemy to their camp at Rathmines. Attacking Ormond's forces before they can form up for battle, Jones comprehensively defeats the coalition forces (2 Aug).
8. Having lost most of his army, Ormond retreats westwards towards Kilkenny (2 Aug).

31

contest between Vaughan's cavaliers and Jones's veteran troopers was uneven and, with their commander falling in the early stages of the mêlée, the Royalist horsemen were soon streaming back towards the main army in disarray. Within the castle, Purcell's infantry resisted as best they could, but outnumbered and surrounded and with their supporting troops routed, the position was untenable and many were either killed or taken prisoner. Rallying his troops on the spot, and surprised at the sudden collapse of the enemy outpost, Jones discerned an opportunity to make his victory complete and gave orders for his small force to advance on Ormond's camp, one and a half kilometres distant.

Awoken by the sound of fighting, Ormond tried to deploy his army for battle but with his lines still in confusion, he was only partially successful this and ordered Colonel John Gifford to advance with Inchiquin's veteran Munster foot and forestall the enemy advance. Had he retained a sizeable mounted reserve, Ormond still might have been able to stabilize his line and salvage the situation, but with two regiments on detachment with Inchiquin and with Vaughan's men in abject flight, this was not an option, and as Gifford's fragmented line closed with the Parliamentarian infantry, its flank and rear quickly became vulnerable to the marauding enemy horsemen and an uneven contest soon became a one-sided slaughter, with the English troopers wreaking havoc amongst the disorganized infantry.

In a last-ditch effort to stop the destruction of his army, Ormond sent an urgent courier to Viscount Dillon at Finglas, ordering him to cross the Liffey and fall upon Jones's rear. Dillon refused to commit his troops to action possibly because he felt that his force was both too small and too distant from the fighting to arrest the Royalist collapse or because he was concerned about being attacked on the march by troops remaining in Dublin.

Looking vainly northwards Ormond soon realized that he could expect no succour from his subordinate and made the decision to quit the field gathering to him as many stragglers as possible. Seeing that there was no hope and unwilling to sacrifice his remaining men for a lost cause, Gifford requested and was granted quarter, and with this surrender the last organized resistance ended and the Royalist camp was overrun.

In his official report to King Charles II, Ormond would perversely describe the battle of Rathmines as a victory, but if so it was a Pyrrhic victory of the most extreme kind – a reasonable estimate of the Royalist casualties would be in the region of 3,500 men killed, to which must then be added the haul of prisoners – 17 field grade officers, 151 officers of lower rank and 2,500 NCOs and other ranks, many of whom would almost immediately swell the ranks of Jones's small army, as well as the army's pay chest and artillery train.

It was the total loss of so much arms and equipment that denoted the depth of the Royalist defeat. Men could be replaced, but without the ability to mass-produce weapons, the Coalition forces were even more than before reliant upon the import of arms and munitions from abroad and whilst odd cargoes could be brought through the enemy blockade, the Commonwealth overwhelming naval superiority meant that there were few gaps in the line through which such clandestine shipments could slip.

Although it had begun as a limited action, Jones's ability to identify and exploit the enemy's mistakes made Rathmines possibly the pivotal engagement of the campaign. With his victory, not only had he guaranteed that Cromwell would have a safe harbour at which to disembark his troops, but in a few short hours he had also ripped the heart out of the Coalition Army. At a single stroke the Royalist war effort had been so badly damaged that Ormond would no longer seek to meet the enemy in open battle, instead he would change his campaign strategy completely and dispose of the majority of his forces in fortifying and garrisoning a number of strategically situated towns and castles, preferring to force the Commonwealth forces to expend their efforts in continuous siege warfare. By continually refusing battle, Hugh Ó Neíll had frustrated the Earl of Essex during the Nine Years War, and Ormond was confident that this tried-and-tested formula would work once again.

## THE COMING OF CROMWELL

After his arrival in Dublin on 15 August, Cromwell immediately went into conference with Jones in order to plan the next stage in the campaign – the re-establishment of land communications with Ulster. Accordingly, and whilst awaiting the bulk of his forces under Ireton, he set about reorganizing the Dublin Army. Despite the fact that its order of battle contained a large number of units, most of Jones's regiments had by now seen several years' continual service in Ireland and, with virtually all of the available manpower being used to reinforce regiments in England, many were at a fraction of their official establishment. Appalled at the indiscipline of the troops, he chose to reduce several of the regiments – those of Borlase, Hungerford, Kynaston, Long and Ponsonby – and use the men thus displaced to fill the ranks of other regiments and bring them up to an approximation of their full strength.

This reorganization also served a secondary purpose by allowing Cromwell to purge the army of a number of officers whom he considered to be either unreliable or unable to fulfil their duties.

Whilst these changes were being implemented Cromwell began a programme of 'hearts and minds'. The majority of Jones's forces had been accustomed to supplying themselves by means of 'free quarter' by which practice they simply took what they needed from the local inhabitants. In order that he not leave a discontented and potentially hostile populace to his rear, Cromwell immediately outlawed this practice stating that any soldiers found guilty of such an abuse would be '… strictly proceeded against and punished according the utmost severity and rigour of the law …'. In order to reinforce this diktat he drew upon the war chest that he had extracted from an unwilling Parliament and ensured that the troops were paid several weeks in advance, with money in their pockets the soldiers could afford to pay for their needs.

Cromwell followed this up by issuing a proclamation to the country as a whole:

> Whereas I am informed that, upon the marching out of the armies heretofore, or of parties from garrisons, a liberty hath been taken by the soldiery to abuse, rob and pillage, and too often to execute cruelties upon the country people: Being resolved, by the Grace of God, diligently and strictly to restrain such wickedness for the future, I do hereby warn and require all officers, soldiers and others under my command, henceforth to forbear all such evil practices as aforesaid, and not to do any wrong or violence towards country people or persons whatsoever, unless they be actually in arms or office with the enemy, and not to meddle with the goods of such without special order.

Armed with a supply of ready coin, and on the assumption that Parliament would continue to be able to meet the cost of field operations, it was a stroke of genius that would go a long way to undermining the regard in which the Coalition forces were held by the very people whom they were supposed to be defending. To emphasize Cromwell's stance on this matter, two private soldiers who had been convicted for theft were paraded in front of the whole army and summarily executed.

Sitting astride the road from Dublin to Belfast where it crossed the river Boyne, it was clear that one of Cromwell's next targets would be the town of Drogheda. With this crucial objective attained, it was assumed that a number of smaller garrisons would fall and thus pave the way for a detached column to secure the route into eastern Ulster. For the next few days, both Cromwell and Jones drilled the army, finally selecting eight regiments of foot and six of horse, totalling some 12,000 men, to form the 'marching army' for use in field operations.

On 31 August, Jones led the advance guard northwards from Dublin, two regiments of horse and Abbott's five troops of dragoons, with Cromwell to follow with the main body on the following day. Here the Parliamentarian commander showed his grasp of the realities of warfare, electing to embark his siege artillery and the bulk of his supplies upon a naval squadron under the command of Sir George Ayscough, which would ascend the Boyne, almost to the walls of Drogheda, where the cannon and munitions would be unloaded and easily transferred to the Parliamentarian camp.

# STREETS RUNNING RED WITH BLOOD, DROGHEDA, 5–11 SEPTEMBER 1649

Although Drogheda's defences had been constructed for a different era of warfare, the town still had the potential to pose a challenge to even the most experienced commander. With an extensive circuit of stone walls some six metres in height and two metres thick at the base, the town was bisected by the river Boyne, the two halves being connected by a single drawbridge at the river's narrowest point.

In accordance with Ormond's intention to bleed the enemy dry in a series of costly sieges, the Coalition's council of war voted unanimously on 23 August that 'Drogheda was to be maintained' and appointed a veteran English soldier, Sir Arthur Aston, to assume command of the garrison. Believing that Drogheda was perfectly suited to this new strategy, Ormond gave instructions that the garrison be strongly reinforced and for sufficient supplies of food and munitions to be laid in to sustain the garrison in the event of the inevitable siege.

The developing consensus amongst the Royalist high command was that not only would it require a considerable force in order to prosecute a conventional siege but that this would be aggravated by the fact that the only two other points which an attacker could use to cross the river and invest the northern half of the town were the ford across the Boyne at Oldbridge a short distance upstream, and the stone bridge at Slane some 13km further west. In short, the view was that if an attacker were to follow the established precepts of siege warfare, a siege of Drogheda would be a long and costly affair. It was a view that would be fatally reflected in the planning of the town's defence.

On 27 August, Aston wrote to Ormond at Tecroghan informing him that whilst attempts were being made to fill the town's magazines with livestock

and foodstuffs drawn in from the local countryside, the most serious deficit was that of munitions. Despite the arrival of a quantity of gunpowder from Dundalk, supplies of match and round shot were almost non-existent, a lack of which would compromise his proposed defence of Drogheda. In the same letter, he offers a piece of intelligence that would have serious consequences for the defenders:

> This morning a gentleman, a near neighbour here, tells me that Jones having summoned all his forces, or of divers adjacent quarters, with what Cromwell brought with him, and all he had before, the muster amounted unto 8000 foot and 4000 horse, and that it is generally believed that they intend their march either tomorrow or at the latest upon Tuesday. It is reported that they intend to divide their army, part to march towards Kilkenny, and the rest to clear (as they call it) these quarters.

It was therefore plain that, although they were aware of the approximate size of Cromwell's force, both Aston and Ormond believed that Drogheda was only a secondary objective, and that the Commonwealth commander intended to make a serious thrust towards Kilkenny with at least half of the forces under his command. In retrospect it would prove to be the first of two fatal mistakes that would greatly contribute to the loss of the town. It is unclear whether significant additional supplies were available or, even if this was the case, they could have been sent to Drogheda before the siege began. What is certain, however, is that there were a number of local garrisons, which, when concentrated, could have posed a threat to Cromwell's flank and lines of communication. Instead of massing his forces, Ormond continued to make suggestions for Aston to dissipate his troops further by ordering that he garrison the small fortalice that covered the bridge at Slane, '... if the Boyne rise it will be necessary to put 15 or 20 men into the castle of the bridge of Slane, which castle stood on the middle of the bridge, and cannot bee taken but with cannon'.

**COMRADES IN ARMS: RATHMINES, 2 AUGUST 1649 (pp. 36–37)**

On the evening of 1 August, Ormond detached a force of 5,000 men under the overall command of Sir Patrick Purcell to fortify the ruins of Baggotrath Castle, which lay between Dublin and the Royalist camp at Rathmines. His intention was to create a strongpoint that would dominate the southern approaches to the city and deny the garrison the use of the pastureland outside the city walls. Unaware that the Dublin garrison had been reinforced by the leading elements of Cromwell's expeditionary force, he was understandably unconcerned by the delays experienced by Purcell's troops, believing that the fortifications would be complete during the course of the following day.

Within the city, Jones decided to disrupt the works at Baggotrath by launching a limited attack, and on the morning of 2 August he assembled a force built around the newly arrived reinforcements and sortied out of the city. The Royalist troops were shattered by the unexpected attack and, with Baggotrath in Commonwealth hands, Jones launched an immediate attack on the enemy units now attempting to form up around their encampment.

In an effort to avert disaster, Ormond rallied what troops he could and threw them into the combat. One of these, Inchiquin's Foot – commanded by Colonel John Gifford – was instrumental in halting Jones's attack, but as his supporting units were gradually driven from the field, Gifford's position became untenable.

Here we see the wounded colonel (1), standing amidst the battered remnants of his regiment (2), hoping to use the fact that he and Jones had previously served together under Ormond as a bargaining counter. He is remonstrating with Jones for his life and those of his men, arguing that as the battle is clearly lost, nothing will be gained by continued fighting.

Jones (3), having been slightly wounded during the engagement, listens intently to his former colleague, weighing up the options. He is conscious of the fact that whilst he has bloodied Ormond's troops and driven them back from the field he has not destroyed them and that when he returns to the city they will come back. Without accurate information about when Cromwell's Army is expected to arrive he is acutely aware that he needs every able-bodied man that he can muster available to fight.

As if aware of this, Gifford, attempts to break the impasse by offering to transfer his allegiance, and those of his men, to Parliament and serve under Jones's command. Whilst the offer is being considered, the tension is compounded by knots of Parliamentarian troopers nervously aiming their weapons at Gifford's men (4) whilst awaiting their general's reaction, unsure if they are facing friend or foe, unsure if the battle is over or if hostilities are merely suspended.

Aston's laconic reply was that if he were to garrison the bridge he might as well consign the troops to being taken prisoner as, if and when the enemy did bring up cannon, the position would have no defence and the men would be captured. In any event, of more importance to him was the crucial fact that the cost of maintaining his forces was far in excess of the agreed contributions that he was able to levy from the surrounding area. Without adequate funds he would be unable to pay the troops and therefore wouldn't necessarily be able to count on them to do their duty. Pleading poverty himself, Ormond continued to promise that Aston's needs would be met.

Despite this wrangling over supplies, and although the rationale was still in the belief that an attack on Drogheda would be only a secondary manoeuvre, Ormond was more constructive in his suggestions that a 'scorched earth' policy be enacted south of the Boyne, and that a number of castles be demolished in order to deny the enemy the possibility of establishing a forward base. A codicil to this suggestion however was the request that Gormanston, Sir Thomas Preston's family estate, be excluded from the planned destruction.

On 2 September, a troop of Royalist cavalry from Drogheda under Captain Finglas encountered the advance elements of Jones's column approaching from Dublin and, greatly outnumbered, were forced to give ground as the Commonwealth troops set up camp some three kilometres south of the town. Aston ordered Finglas to remain in contact with the enemy and report their numbers and intent, but Jones forced him to withdraw by pushing a regiment of horse across the Boyne at Oldbridge. The following day, Cromwell arrived with the remainder of the army, and for the first time Aston realized that the enemy had not split as had been believed and that the bulk of the Commonwealth force was now deployed before Drogheda, some 12,000 men against the 2,500 or so men taking shelter behind the walls. Whilst confident in the conduct of the four infantry regiments that made up the core of his garrison – the Lord Lieutenant's, Byrne's, Wall's and Warren's – Aston was less sanguine about the fighting ability of the independent troops of horse, but consoled himself with the fact that once the town was invested the cavalrymen would have to fight, having no other option.

Despite the disparity in numbers, Aston decided to mount an aggressive defence as a means of boosting the garrison's morale, sending out regular patrols to harass the enemy. Without further tangible support from Ormond, however, this would prove to be a policy of self-destruction. When Aston took command at Drogheda, he recorded that the town's magazine had contained a mere 55 barrels of powder, and now with the enemy closing in this precious commodity was being used up at a rate of four barrels a day. Simply put, without succour from Ormond, the town's supply of powder would run out by 16 September at the latest – sooner if the troops were called upon to repulse a major enemy attack.

As the noose began to tighten Aston received a final reinforcement from Ormond in the form of Lieutenant-Colonel Griffin Kavenagh and a detachment of 500 men from the garrison of Trim. At the same time, the Commonwealth heavy cannon had arrived and, after being unloaded a short distance downstream from Drogheda, they were escorted into the siege lines and deployed in previously sited batteries. With his forces finally concentrated Cromwell could now begin to plan his operations in earnest.

The following day Aston sent Ormond a final plea for assistance, 'I gave Your Excellency notice of two sallies which I made upon the enemy, which proved both successful and advantageous; as also I informed Your Excellency

Lieutenant-Colonel Daniel Axtell. The involvement of Hewson's close friend and former apprentice in the suspicious train of events at Mill Mount casts some doubt upon Cromwell's role in the massacre. (Courtesy of the National Portrait Gallery, London)

Colonel John Hewson. A capable officer, this former cobbler and zealous lay preacher, was representative of the more extreme religious elements within the ranks of the New Model Army. (Courtesy of the National Gallery of Ireland. Photo © National Gallery of Ireland)

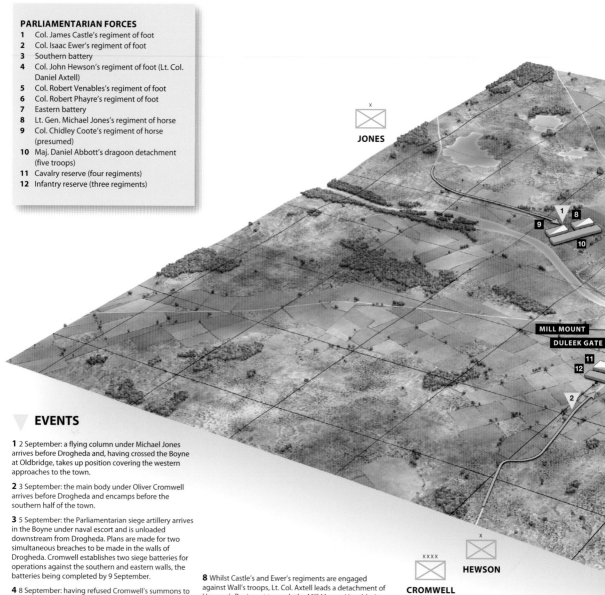

**PARLIAMENTARIAN FORCES**
1. Col. James Castle's regiment of foot
2. Col. Isaac Ewer's regiment of foot
3. Southern battery
4. Col. John Hewson's regiment of foot (Lt. Col. Daniel Axtell)
5. Col. Robert Venables's regiment of foot
6. Col. Robert Phayre's regiment of foot
7. Eastern battery
8. Lt. Gen. Michael Jones's regiment of horse
9. Col. Chidley Coote's regiment of horse (presumed)
10. Maj. Daniel Abbott's dragoon detachment (five troops)
11. Cavalry reserve (four regiments)
12. Infantry reserve (three regiments)

JONES

MILL MOUNT
DULEEK GATE

HEWSON

CROMWELL

### ▼ EVENTS

**1** 2 September: a flying column under Michael Jones arrives before Drogheda and, having crossed the Boyne at Oldbridge, takes up position covering the western approaches to the town.

**2** 3 September: the main body under Oliver Cromwell arrives before Drogheda and encamps before the southern half of the town.

**3** 5 September: the Parliamentarian siege artillery arrives in the Boyne under naval escort and is unloaded downstream from Drogheda. Plans are made for two simultaneous breaches to be made in the walls of Drogheda. Cromwell establishes two siege batteries for operations against the southern and eastern walls, the batteries being completed by 9 September.

**4** 8 September: having refused Cromwell's summons to surrender, the garrison commander, Sir Arthur Aston, moves his command post to the Mill Mount in the southern half of the town. Sir Edmund Verney assumes command of the northern half of the town.

**5** 9 September: the Parliamentarian bombardment of Drogheda begins.

**6** 11 September: the walls of Drogheda are breached in two places by the Parliamentarian siege artillery.

**7** 11th September: at 5.00pm Cromwell gives the order to storm Drogheda. The initial assaults are heavily repulsed by Wall's Royalist foot. Colonel James Castle is killed leading his regiment against the southern breach. Parliamentarian assault columns are heavily reinforced, and a second attack succeeds in clearing both breaches, killing Col. Wall whose regiment recoils with some men fleeing for the drawbridge across the Boyne, and some for the relative safety of Mill Mount.

**8** Whilst Castle's and Ewer's regiments are engaged against Wall's troops, Lt. Col. Axtell leads a detachment of Hewson's Regiment towards the Mill Mount. Venables's and Phayre's regiments enter Drogheda through the eastern breach. The Duleek Gate is forced, and the Parliamentarian reserve begins to enter the town.

**9** Axtell surrounds Sir Arthur Aston's command post on Mill Mount and summons the Royalist commander to surrender. Aston surrenders but he and his men are killed after first being disarmed by Axtell's troops. Indiscriminate killing of garrison troops by Parliamentarian forces now begins. Numbers of civilians are caught up in the bloodshed.

**10** Royalist troops fail to raise the drawbridge across the Boyne, Parliamentarian troops flood into the northern half of the town, eliminating isolated pockets of resistance. Cromwell orders St Peter's Church, occupied by civilians as well as enemy troops, to be burnt down. Fighting in Drogheda slowly comes to an end as the final Royalist positions are taken by the Parliamentarian troops.

# THE SIEGE OF DROGHEDA

The events of September 1649 showing the movements of the Parliamentarian forces under Oliver Cromwell as they besiege and assault the town of Drogheda.

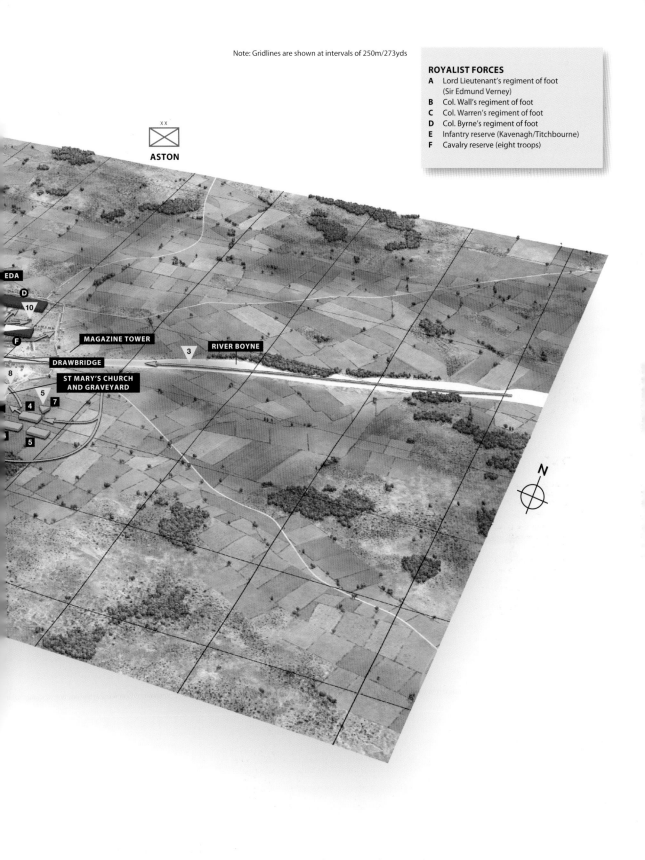

Note: Gridlines are shown at intervals of 250m/273yds

**ASTON**

**ROYALIST FORCES**

A Lord Lieutenant's regiment of foot
 (Sir Edmund Verney)
B Col. Wall's regiment of foot
C Col. Warren's regiment of foot
D Col. Byrne's regiment of foot
E Infantry reserve (Kavenagh/Titchbourne)
F Cavalry reserve (eight troops)

EDA

D

10

F

MAGAZINE TOWER

RIVER BOYNE

3

DRAWBRIDGE

ST MARY'S CHURCH
AND GRAVEYARD

8

5  7

4

5

N

Drogheda, looking down into the ravine from the eastern walls. The area that sheltered Hewson's Brigade prior to it launching an uphill attack on the second breach can be easily discerned at the junction of the descending pathways on either side of the tree at the centre of the image. (Author's collection)

that my ammunition was far spent, each day having cost me since Sunday last four barrels, by keeping the enemy from working and with sallies. My provisions grow short and [I have] not a penny of money.' He continued by again requesting that Ormond make some form of demonstration against the enemy camp, which he would support with the garrison of Drogheda.

Rather than acting conventionally as both Ormond and Aston had believed he would, Cromwell now decided to invest the southern half of the town whilst simultaneously enforcing a loose blockade of the northern sector. In effect he would allow himself the luxury of massing his forces at the chosen point of assault whilst simultaneously ensuring that the enemy would be diluted by the need to man the whole defensive perimeter in anticipation of secondary attacks. With a cavalryman's eye for terrain, he sited his batteries so that they would have converging fields of fire against the southern and south-eastern walls of Drogheda, giving the attacking forces the potential of creating breaches at two separate but mutually supporting points. Another important factor in his positioning of the siege artillery was that Drogheda's eastern wall was buttressed by a steep ravine wherein the attacking troops could take shelter out of range of enemy small arms until the order was given to assault the breach.

The Commonwealth plan of attack was simple, and followed a set pattern that had been employed by both sides during the Civil War. Firstly, the walls would be bombarded until at least one 'practicable' breach had been achieved, i.e. one which it was felt could be successfully stormed. At this point the town would be summoned to surrender. Should the town governor elect to continue to resist, the breaches would be assaulted with a number of troops being detailed to seize and open the town gate. Once this objective was secured, the cavalry massed opposite would then launch an attack through the open gate, their instructions being to ride for the town square – the most likely area for the enemy commander to have concentrated both his reserves and his

headquarters. Although cavalry were particularly vulnerable within built-up areas, it was felt that this was countered by the speed with which they could neutralize the enemy's command structure and disrupt his deployment of reserves to threatened sectors. If the defender's surrender could be forced quickly enough, it had the potential to significantly reduce the casualties taken by the attacking units.

Given the fact that Cromwell planned to breach Drogheda's walls in two adjacent sectors, it is reasonable to assume that this tactic was refined slightly in that troops attacking the southern wall were detailed to secure the Duleek Gate thus facilitating the entry of the cavalry reserve, whereas the troops assaulting the eastern breach had been ordered to push on into Drogheda and capture the drawbridge across the Boyne, thus securing egress into the northern half of the town.

**TOP**
Interior close-up of the extreme south-eastern corner of Drogheda's town walls. Cromwell's plan called for converging artillery fire not only to breach the wall in two places, but also to render this section of the defences untenable, thus making the storming of the breach that much easier by removing the threat from one of the attacking columns' flanks. (Author's collection)

**BOTTOM**
Drogheda, close-up of the head of the ravine as seen from the eastern walls, showing the dead ground in which Axtell was able to rally Hewson's regiment after it had been repulsed in the initial assault. The steepness of the slope effectively sheltered the troops and allowed them to re-form unmolested by enemy fire. (Author's collection)

**OPPOSITE PAGE**
Drogheda, 11 September 1649. In this depiction of the second Commonwealth assault as seen from the Royalist positions, James Castle's Regiment has stormed across the southern breach. The usage, in hand-to-hand combat, of clubbed muskets in preference to swords was common to both armies. (Artist Seán Ó Brógáin, courtesy of the Millmount Museum, Drogheda)

The army was therefore to be divided into three smaller forces; Jones would take the remainder of the advance guard across the Boyne to operate against the northern part of Drogheda, pinning down as many of the defenders as possible, whilst Colonel John Hewson would assume overall command of the three regiments of foot that had been detailed to assault the eastern breach – Daniel Axtell (*vice* Hewson), Robert Phayre and Robert Venables. The remainder of the army would be under Cromwell's direct command – the cavalry opposite the Duleek Gate, with the regiments of

The interior of the eastern breach at Drogheda, overrun by the regiments of Hewson, Venables and Phayre. The majority of the gravestones pre-date the siege of 1649 and may indicate that this area was relatively open at the time of the assault. Later repairs to the stonework can easily be seen in the middle section of the wall. (Author's collection)

James Castle and Isaac Ewer deployed to their right flank in position to attack the southern wall, with the remaining troops being retained as a general reserve to reinforce whichever sector made the most progress.

For two days the heavy artillery played upon the defences, eventually breaching the wall at two points, one each side of the south-eastern corner of the town. As a counter to this, once the intended targets of the inevitable attack became clear and, leaving his deputy, Sir Edmund Verney (son and namesake of King Charles I's standard bearer at Edgehill), in command of the northern sector, Aston moved his command post south of the Boyne to the Mill Mount, site of an Anglo-Norman motte and easily Drogheda's most prominent terrain feature. He then ordered Colonel Wall in command of the southern defences to begin the construction of a line of trenches for use as a secondary line of defence should the main wall prove to be untenable. As a final measure, some of the independent troops of horse were then moved into the southern part of Drogheda as a reaction force to counter any sudden enemy breakthrough.

With the wall breached, Cromwell ordered a white flag to be raised above his command tent, to signify his desire to parley, and at 8.00am on 10 September sent an officer to Aston with a summons to surrender: 'Having brought the army belonging to the Parliament of England before this place to reduce it to obedience, to the end that effusion of blood may be prevented, I thought fit to summon you to deliver the same into my hands to their use. If this be refused you will have no reason to blame me.'

The message was unequivocal, that Aston either immediately surrendered or Cromwell would order a general assault. In itself, the summons was not a declaration that no quarter would be granted to the defenders should the assault be successful, but Cromwell was in no mind for lengthy discussions.

An extreme close-up of the interior of the eastern breach at Drogheda, clearly showing detail of the repairs undertaken on the orders of Colonel John Hewson after his appointment as military governor of Drogheda. (Author's collection)

Encouraged by his previous correspondence, and still believing that there was a chance of relief, Aston refused the summons and, as he wrote that evening in one of his last letters to Ormond:

> This morning at about 8 of the clock, I received the enclosed summons. ... Since this summons I heard no answer but by the mouth of cannon, that which hath ever since without intermission played upon our walls and works. They have eight pieces of battery, the least thereof shoot 12lb [and] one of 30lb bullet. They have made a very great breach near the church and I am confident their resolutions are to gain it immediately by assault.
>
> The soldiers may well, pray God, do well and I assure Your Excellency that there shall be no want in me, but Your Excellency's speedy help is much desired ...

Cromwell immediately ordered the bombardment intensified and by noon the following day, 11 September, the eight heavy cannon had fired almost 300 round shot at the walls, which by now were crumbling badly under the relentless bombardment. At about 5.00pm Cromwell decided that the breaches were both 'practicable' and ordered an assault to be made.

The leading regiments – Castle's and Hewson's – initially made good progress and a number of men gained a precarious foothold in the town; Castle's men also seized the ruins of a small outlier or '*tenalia*' on the southern wall, but were unable to exploit their success as the sally port that led from it into the town was blocked both by rubble and a number of enemy dead. But before the attackers could reorganize themselves a devastating close-range volley of musketry and swift counterattack by Wall's troops ejected them from the spill, their morale faltering as Castle fell mortally wounded. As Hewson was later to write in his account of the fighting: '... we entered

**CROMWELL'S MASTERPIECE: DROGHEDA, 11 SEPTEMBER 1649 (pp. 48–49)**

Bisected by the river Boyne, and compromised by the mistaken belief that Cromwell would divide his army for field operations, many considered the Royalist position at Drogheda to be an exceptionally strong one.

On his arrival before the town, Cromwell decided to attack the defences at two separate points which would not only stretch the defending forces but, choosing to assault the south-eastern corner of the town, it would allow him to use converging batteries against the target area thereby maximizing the damage caused by his siege artillery – exemplified not only by the shattered walls but also by the damaged structure of St Mary's Church, which was literally caught in the crossfire. Another innovation in Cromwell's planning was the use of the 'Dale', a steep ravine that runs along the eastern flank of the defences as a staging area in which a number of his troops can form up for the attack, sheltered from enemy fire.

Here we see the view from the headquarters of Colonel John Hewson (1), in command of the attack on the eastern wall at the time of the second – and successful – assault on Drogheda.

Whilst Hewson confers with a number of his officers the brigade, led by his own regiment under the command of Lieutenant-Colonel Daniel Axtell, is forming up in the safety of the ravine (2), whilst above their heads the eastern siege battery fires a few last rounds at the breach in order to prevent the enemy from manning their defences (3).

Along the southern wall, and following the death of Colonel James Castle who had been killed in the first attack, Cromwell personally leads the remnants of Castle's men, supported by Ewer's regiment to clear the enemy from the breach and break into the town (4). It is a critical decision as, whilst his presence steadies the troops and encourages them to greater efforts, the army commander is literally unable to command the army at a crucial stage in the fighting.

Further along the southern wall, and in keeping with what had developed as standard practice, the Commonwealth horse (5) are waiting – out of range of enemy small arms – for a detachment of troops to seize the Duleek Gate from within, their task being to charge into the town and disrupt the movement of enemy reserves.

the breach, but not so orderly as was appointed, we were stoutly resisted and after a short dispute, did retreat disorderly, tumbling over the breach and down a steep hill that ascends up to the wall …'.

The supports were then ordered forward in an attempt to regain the momentum, Cromwell himself personally advancing at the head of Ewer's Regiment whilst Axtell, in command of the assault on the eastern breach and rallying his men in the bottom of the ravine, was more than content to see Phayre and Venables moving forwards to his aid. Above his head the heavy guns again opened fire on the breach, enfilading the enemy position and wreaking havoc amongst the defenders.

Inspired by the Lord General's presence, the assaulting parties again swarmed over the rubble, closing with the enemy in a flurry of swords and clubbed muskets. This time the Royalist counterattack was unsuccessful, with Colonel Wall being killed in the confused mêlée and the defenders being steadily pushed back across their retrenchments. To the east, Axtell again led his men up the slope but this time, shattered by the artillery fire, there was no coherent defence and the three regiments of Parliamentarian foot entered the breach, fanning out and outflanking the heavily outnumbered defenders.

With increasing numbers of enemy troops now pouring into Drogheda, the Royalist position was spiralling out of control. Aston attempted to stabilize the situation by ordering the two reserve troops of horse forward, but in doing so he uncovered the drawbridge and the enemy troops poured into the resulting gap. Phayre and Venables headed towards the river whilst Axtell had identified another target for himself, Aston's command post on the Mill Mount.

Starkly imposing, with its steep slopes and walled terraces, the fortified enclosure could be approached only by a narrow causeway wide enough for only two men to travel abreast. And now, defended not only by Aston's headquarters staff but by a large number of refugees from Wall's Regiment, its capture would be a formidable task indeed.

'A tough nut to crack' – a sketch of the Mill Mount as it would most likely have appeared during the siege. Note the curtain wall and small towers lining the base of the hill. (Courtesy Seán Ó Brógáin, after Thomas Phillips, 1685)

As they assaulted into the eastern breach, overrunning the few remaining defenders, Axtell's men stormed through this small chapel before outflanking Colonel Wall's defensive positions and driving towards Aston's headquarters on the Mill Mount. (Author's collection)

Having surrounded the base of the hill, Axtell then sent an officer to request a parley with Aston, a request that was fatefully accepted and, a short time later, Axtell himself ascended the mount for an interview with the Royalist commander. What exactly was discussed between the two men will most probably never be known, but the result was that Aston and his small force left the protection of their defences and were then taken into custody and disarmed by Axtell's men who, in the following moments set in motion the train of events that led to one of the most controversial events in Irish history. Within minutes, most of Aston's men were either dead or dying, whilst their commander himself lay bleeding on the flagstones, bludgeoned to death with his wooden leg, seized from him by soldiers in the belief that it contained money and precious stones.

Under the terms of the commonly accepted 'rules of war' of the period, it was acknowledged that troops who were offered quarter after having fought on after a summons to surrender were entitled to their lives only and that their personal effects were deemed to be part of the victor's spoils; it is possible, therefore, that a dispute broke out over the possession of a trinket or bauble and that, fired by the tensions of combat, religious prejudice or a number of causes, what may have started out as a simple scuffle degenerated eventually leading to violence and bloodshed. Another plausible explanation may lie in the character of Axtell himself. Extreme in his religious beliefs, he nursed a deep hatred of the Catholic church and it could be that he simply treated with Aston in order to lure him out of his defences before ordering his men to kill the unarmed prisoners; indeed he would perform a similar

# Cromwell seizes the initiative, September–December 1649

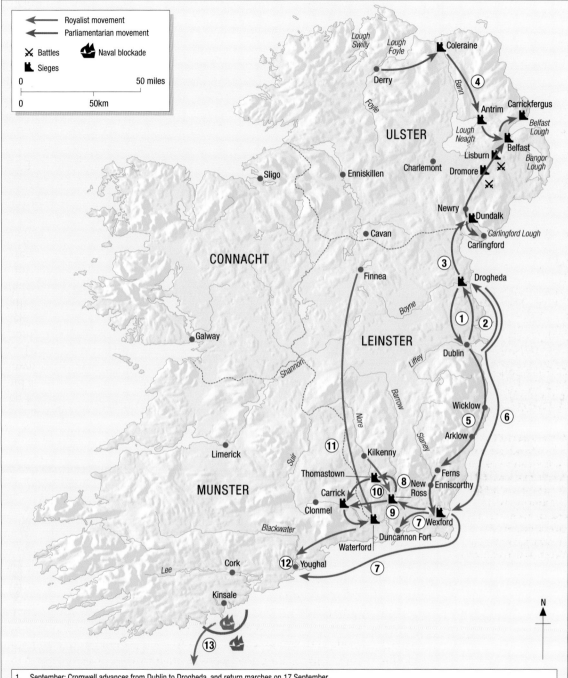

1. September: Cromwell advances from Dublin to Drogheda, and return marches on 17 September.
2. The Parliamentarian heavy artillery moves from Dublin to Drogheda by sea. Batteries are quickly established and the walls breached on 10 September. Drogheda is stormed on 11 September.
3. Colonel Robert Venables is ordered to march north with two regiments of foot (Venables, Fenwick) and one of horse (Chidley Coote) and pacify Eastern Ulster.
4. Sir Charles Coote marches from Derry to assist Venables in Eastern Ulster.
5. 23 September: Cromwell marches from Dublin to Wexford, where he arrives on 1 October.
6. The Parliamentarian heavy artillery moves from Dublin to Wexford by sea. The town falls to assault on 11 October.
7. 16 October: a detachment under Henry Ireton is sent to capture Duncannon Fort. Broghill is sent to rally parliamentary support in Munster.
8. 17 October: Cromwell moves to besiege New Ross, which has been reinforced by Royalist troops under Sir Lucas Taaffe.
9. 19 October: New Ross surrenders.
10. 19 November: detachments under Michael Jones and John Reynolds are detailed to capture Carrick and Thomastown. Cromwell approaches Waterford from the north-west on 24 November.
11. 30 November : 1,500 troops from Ó Neill's Army of Ulster arrive to reinforce the garrison of Waterford. Richard Farrell assumes governorship of the city.
12. December: Cromwell sends his army into winter quarters.
13. December: bad weather disrupts the Parliamentarian blockade of Kinsale and allows Rupert's ships to slip out to sea, eventually heading for Portugal.

In this interior view of St Mary's Churchyard, the construction details of the southern town wall, such as buttresses and walkways, can be easily discerned. The obelisk, which is about two metres high provides a useful guide to the height of the defensive works. (Author's collection)

deception at Meelick in 1652 when he offered quarter to a detachment of Clanricarde's troops and as soon as their surrender had been taken, ordered his men to kill them out of hand. Whatever the exact cause, the cry of 'no quarter!' soon reverberated through the ranks of the Commonwealth soldiers, and many small groups of prisoners found themselves put up against a wall and, as was euphemistically termed at the time, 'knocked on the head'.

Unopposed, the Parliamentarian troops now flooded across the drawbridge, and into the northern part of the town, killing indiscriminately and swamping the enemy by sheer weight of numbers. Resistance was quickly limited to a few isolated redoubts such at the bell tower of St Peter's Church, and some of the gatehouses and towers on the northern circuit of the walls. Having been caught up in the hand-to-hand combat in St Mary's Churchyard, and perhaps caught up by the madness of an army that is unleashed on a town, when Cromwell began to reassert his command and was asked what should be done about the defenders of St Peter's, he simply gave orders that the wooden pews be gathered around the tower and the enemy burnt out. A number managed to escape the conflagration but were immediately killed, whilst the remainder, as many as 40 men, stayed put and perished in the flames. Seeing the fate of their comrades, the troops in the towers capitulated trusting on Cromwell's mercy. Many, including all of their officers, were immediately executed, whilst the remainder were earmarked for deportation as slave labour on Barbados and other Caribbean islands. With night falling the killing continued, with reports of prisoners – including Sir Edmund Verney, Aston's deputy, and a number of senior Royalist officers – being executed some days after the sack.

Readily acknowledged by friend and foe alike as being an extremely devout man, the fact that Cromwell readily ascribed his victory to divine providence has given his conduct the undertones of a war of religious extermination, something which becomes more understandable when set in context against the actions and opinions of a number of the more extreme officers such as Hewson and Axtell who, whilst brave and capable men, were also unscrupulous in their dealings with those whom they viewed as religious subversives, whether Catholic, Presbyterian or any other confessional grouping that didn't fall in line with their particular brand of politico-religious fervour.

Cromwell himself describes the events at Drogheda, in a letter dated 16 September to John Bradshaw, chairman of the Council of State, he wrote: '... we refused them quarter, having the day before summoned the town. I

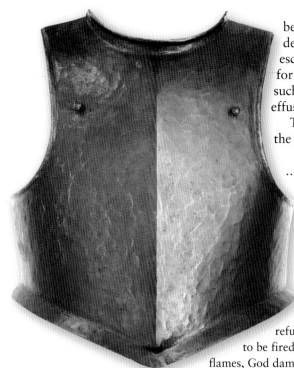

This close-up of a cavalry trooper's breastplate shows in great detail the manufacturing technique used to produce the fitted metal but also the mark of a 'proofing shot' just below the collar, so called as it signified that the armour was 'proof' against small-arms fire. (Courtesy of the Trustees, Royal Armouries, Leeds)

believe we put to the sword the whole number of the defendants. I do not think thirty of the whole number escaped with their lives, those that did are in safe custody for Barbadoes. ... The enemy were filled upon this with such terror, and I truly believe this bitterness will save much effusion of blood, through the goodness of God.'

The following day, in his official report to the Speaker of the House of Commons he described events at Mill Mount:

... our men getting up to them, were ordered by me to put them all to the sword; and indeed being in the heat of action, I forbade them to spare any that were in arms in the town, and I think that night they put to the sword about two thousand men, divers of the officers and soldiers being fled over the bridge into the other part of the town, where about one hundred of them possessed St Peter's Church steeple, some the west gate, and others, a round strong tower next to the gate, called St Sunday's: These being summoned to yield to mercy, refused; whereupon I ordered the steeple of St Peter's Church to be fired, where one of them was heard to say in the midst of the flames, God damn me, God confound me, I burn, I burn; the next day the other two towers were summoned, in one of which was about six or seven score, but they refused to yield themselves; and we knowing that hunger must compel them set only good guards to secure them from running away, until their [empty] stomacks [forced them to] come down from one of the said towers, notwithstanding their condition, they killed and wounded some of our men; when they submitted, their officers were knockt on the head, and every tenth man of the soldiers killed, and the rest shipped for the Barbadoes; the soldiers in the other tower were all spared, as to their lives only, and shipped likewise for the Barbadoes. I am persuaded that this is a righteous judgement of God upon these barbarous wretches, who have imbued their hands in so much innocent blood, and that it will tend to prevent the effusion of blood for the future, which are the satisfactory grounds to such actions, which otherwise cannot but work remorse and regret ...

Cromwell then gives a narrative of his actions following the sack of Drogheda, and adds:

... and now give me leave to say how it comes to pass that this work was wrought; it was set upon some of our hearts that a great thing should be done, not by power, or might, but by the Spirit of God; and is it not so clear? That which caused your men to storm so courageously, it was the Spirit of God, who gave your men courage, and took it away again, and the enemy courage, and took it away again, and gave your men courage again, and therewith this happy success; and therefore it is good that God alone have all the glory ...

With Drogheda in Commonwealth hands, Cromwell now began to prepare for the next stage of the campaign – using the threat of similar violence as was meted out in Drogheda, he sent flying columns to Dundalk and Trim to summon each stronghold to surrender. His summons to the commander of Dundalk, dated 12 September, reads:

This common version of Cromwell's entry into Drogheda during the sack. The dour, Puritan commander is seen looking on unconcerned, cold and unemotional whilst members of the New Model Army murder defenceless civilians in cold blood. A useful propaganda tool this style of image has gone a long way to developing the perception of the sack of Drogheda as being an act of deliberate policy. (Courtesy of Mary Evans Picture Library)

> ... I offered mercy to the garrison of Treedagh (Drogheda), in sending the Governor a summons before I attempted the taking of it. Which being refused brought their evil upon them. If you, being warned thereby, shall surrender your garrison to the use of the Parliament of England, which by this I summon you to do, you may thereby prevent effusion of blood.
>
> If, upon refusing this offer, that which you like not befalls you, you will know whom to blame ...

Almost invariably compared with the contemporary sack of Magdeburg by Catholic Imperialist troops under Count van Tilly in 1630, the question which needs to be asked is to what degree is Cromwell implicated in the slaughter that took place in Drogheda on 11 September 1649, and the succeeding few days? Opinion is readily divided into those who believe that the killing was an act of deliberate anti-Irish or anti-Catholic policy on Cromwell's part, whilst others maintain that he was simply acting within the remit of the 'rules of war' that were commonly accepted during the period. These distinct camps can be readily ascertained by the titles of two recent works dealing with his campaign in Ireland – *God's Executioner* and *Cromwell, an Honourable Enemy*.

A plausible explanation is that when Axtell had Aston and his men killed, Cromwell was still embroiled in the fighting around St Mary's Churchyard (the southern breach) and as such was incapable of exerting any command over his army, especially over an army ripe with religious tension and frustration at the fact that, despite successive defeats in England, the Royalists simply would not acknowledge that the war was at an end and continued to foment what they viewed as treason and unrest. By the time that order of sorts had been restored, it was too late and the wave of killing had begun.

When tempers had cooled Cromwell would have been faced with a difficult decision. On one hand, should he accept responsibility for the conduct of the troops under his command or on the other, should he rather choose to discipline a number of his senior officers for theirs; conduct with which the bulk of his army would have had complete and total sympathy.

In effect, and whilst conveniently ignoring the fact that a significant number of Aston's garrison were his co-religionists, what Cromwell does in his accounts of the siege is to divide the occupants of the town neatly into denominational groups, implying that Protestants were a minority in Drogheda rather than the majority and citing the fact that in the days prior to the assault they had been denied the right to practice their faith, thereby ascribing the subsequent fate of Drogheda to divine displeasure. Aston may have been as staunch in his religious beliefs as Cromwell was in his, but given his experience as a soldier it is difficult to believe that he would have risked aggravating the existing rifts between the Catholic and Protestant troops under his command in the certain knowledge that he would need all of his troops in the coming engagement.

In the final analysis, the choice was not a difficult one for him to make. And in his official correspondence, he accepts full responsibility for the massacre, establishing a terrible future precedent for other enemy garrisons that may choose to ignore the warning of Drogheda.

In Cromwell's own words '... it will tend to prevent the effusion of blood for the future ...'

Backsword, 'mortuary' style, English *c.*1640. The most common type of cavalry sword, the blade of this example is inscribed *Me Fecit Hounsloe*, indicating its place of manufacture, Hounslow in Middlesex. (Courtesy of the Trustees, Royal Armouries, Leeds)

The alternative would not only have been to risk discontent in the army at a time when its main tactical advantage was its cohesion and discipline, but it would also have called into question his suitability for the Irish command, especially if it could be shown to have lost control over the army in its first major engagement. What ought not to be forgotten is that at this time, Cromwell was simply one lieutenant-general amongst a number of officers of similar rank in the Commonwealth army and that whilst, through patronage and family ties, he could count on a number of allies amongst them, there were also a number of rivals and opponents who would have had no qualms about taking advantage of any mistakes he may have made.

# CONSOLIDATION

In the aftermath of Drogheda, Cromwell's most pressing need was to clear a number of outlying enemy garrisons, a task in which he was aided both by rumours spread by fugitives escaping the town and by the adoption of a harsher attitude in demanding the surrender of enemy garrisons. Whilst his summons to Aston reflected purely the form of such a demand, those to Trim, Dundalk and a series of other towns displayed the stark reality of what resistance would mean. Unwilling to share the fate of their compatriots, many local commanders elected to decamp and leave the civilians to their fate.

To the west, Ormond reorganized what remained of his forces in an attempt to salvage what he could from the fruits of two military disasters. Cromwell dispatched Venables with a small column to clear the route into Ulster and commence joint operations with Sir Charles Coote in Derry to bring the province under Commonwealth control. He himself, after leaving a garrison in Drogheda under Hewson, returned to Dublin in order to take care of his wounded and prepare for the next stage of the campaign. There he was relieved to find that Horton's regiment of horse had finally landed, thus offsetting the loss of the unit that had been sent north with Venables.

Ulick Burke, 1st Marquess of Clanricarde. One of the few Catholic magnates who adhered to the Crown during the Rising of 1641, Clanricarde commanded the Coalition forces in Connacht with varying success, his forces eventually being decimated by Axtell at Meelick Island in 1652. (Courtesy of the National Gallery of Ireland, Dublin)

At this point, Cromwell's options were twofold. Counting upon the fact that as a result of the defeats at Rathmines and Drogheda, the enemy had not only lost several thousand of their best troops but also an almost prohibitive amount of arms and equipment, he could take the field army westwards, threatening Kilkenny in the hope of enticing Ormond to give battle in order to save his capital, or he could strike southwards along the coast and in a rapid campaign seize the principal enemy ports in the provinces of Leinster and Munster, severing Ormond's most direct route of communications with his supporters on the Continent, and in addition clearing out several nests of privateers who were the scourge of English merchantmen. Moving along the coast also meant that he would always be within reach of naval support and, more importantly that supplies and heavy artillery could be transported by sea.

In the opposite camp, Ormond's coalition was beginning to falter, with several districts now refusing to make contributions to a cause that seemed already lost and he elected to reinforce a number of garrisons in order to slow down the enemy advance whilst creating a mobile force of some 3,000 men with which he intended to operate against small enemy detachments.

The Commonwealth Army left Dublin on 23 September with the town of Wexford as its objective, the capture of which would mean that, following Venables' success in Ulster, the whole of Ireland's eastern seaboard would lie in Parliamentarian hands. As the army marched out, the Lord General gave another chilling reminder that he was a man of his word when he ordered that a number of soldiers who had broken his provisions on looting be publicly hanged. Whilst on one hand it was a welcome act of reassurance to the local populace, on the other it was a message to the enemy underlining Cromwell's implacability.

By 1 October, the army reached Wexford. En route, many of the Royalist garrisons had simply decamped, and the only occasions when its march was contested were when it had to move away from the coast and was ambushed crossing the Wicklow Hills, south of Arklow, and when the army had to force a crossing over the river Slaney at Enniscorthy.

Never taken by direct assault, Duncannon Fort would remain a Royalist stronghold until the surrender of Waterford rendered its position untenable. As seen from the beach below, this view of the complex clearly shows the strength of the position at the head of a narrow peninsula jutting into the Barrow Estuary. (Kieran Laffan)

## THE CONSEQUENCE OF RESISTANCE, WEXFORD, 2–11 OCTOBER 1649

The site of the second of Cromwell's major sieges in Ireland could not have been more different from the first. Situated on the southern side of the Slaney estuary, the town of Wexford occupied a far stronger defensive position than Drogheda. Covered by a circuit of substantial medieval defences reinforced with an earthen embankment, a small castle buttressed the town's south wall whilst its eastern flank was rendered inviolate from direct attack by a large bay that opened out into the estuary, itself shielded by a southwards-pointing peninsula from which the heavy cannon of Rosslare Fort controlled access to the harbour, preventing any junction between the army and its naval support.

Marching south from Enniscorthy, as the column of 6,000 Parliamentarian troops crossed the Slaney and began to move into position covering the western approaches to the town it appeared to many that Ormond's Fabian tactics had in fact been vindicated. As part of his policy of strengthening garrisons likely to be attacked by the enemy, Ormond had, shortly before Cromwell's arrival, sent Lieutenant-Colonel David Sinnott to Wexford with over a thousand infantry, ordering him to assume command of the garrison, thereby bringing the number of troops manning the defences to 4,500 men.

On 3 October, Cromwell formally initiated the siege by sending Sinnott a summons to surrender the town:

> … having brought the army belonging to the Parliament of England before this place to reduce it to its due obedience, to the end effusion of blood may be prevented, and this town and country about it preserved from ruin, I thought fit to summon you to deliver the same into my hands, to the use of the State of England; by this offer, I hope it will clearly appear where the guilt will lie, if innocent persons should come to suffer with the guilty …

Again, the veiled threat was there, but this time the garrison neither fled nor capitulated.

It is unclear whether Sinnott was confident in his ability to hold out until relieved and was simply playing for time or whether he misunderstood Cromwell's resolution, but his response was hardly calculated to be accepted by the Commonwealth general:

> … I have received your letter of summons, for the delivery up of this town into your hands, which standeth not with my honour to do of myself: neither will I take it upon me without the advice of the rest of the officers, and Mayor of this Corporation, this town being of so great consequence to all Ireland, whom I will call together, and confer with, and return my resolution unto you tomorrow by 12 of the clock: in the mean time, if you be so pleased, I am content to forbear all acts of hostility, so you admit no approach to be made …

The response was swift and unequivocal, Cromwell courteously granted Sinnott until the following day in order to confer with the civil and military authorities, but refused point blank to suspend military operations. As if to underline this point, Michael Jones led a mixed force against Rosslare Fort, which fell without a shot being fired when the garrison fled in the face of the advancing troops.

Despite what many would have viewed as a major setback – the enemy could now bring their warships up to Wexford and, more importantly land

This close-up of Duncannon Fort shows clearly how the advent of gunpowder weapons had begun to affect fortress design. Walls were now thicker and more squat to absorb the impact of enemy shot whilst they were also often angled to deflect incoming cannon balls. (Kieran Laffan)

the siege artillery – for the next few days Sinnott continued to treat with Cromwell as if he held the advantage, but these talks were temporarily suspended when Castlehaven was able to slip 500 men across the Slaney and into the town. Despite this final reinforcement, time was running out for the defenders. On 9 October, Ormond made a thrust against the siege lines from his base at New Ross but despite his numerical superiority, when Jones came north with 15 troops of horse and three of dragoons, he aborted the attack and withdrew on Kilkenny. Wexford was now completely isolated.

Throughout all this, correspondence was still passing between besiegers and besieged when, early in the afternoon of 11 October, Cromwell's siege guns breached the walls of Wexford castle in three places, and it was at this time that Wexford's fate was sealed. By now aware, like Aston had been at Drogheda, that there would be no relief, Sinnott finally requested surrender terms.

Pragmatic, Cromwell was more than aware of the amount of military stores held in the town and, in order to secure it for his own future use and, despite having earlier denied another list of Sinnott's demands, was now more than prepared to be extraordinarily lenient. In return for immediate surrender, he would guarantee the lives and property of the citizens of Wexford in addition to which the garrison would be granted quarter 'for their lives' and having surrendered their arms and equipment would be permitted to return unmolested to their homes on condition that they never again bear arms against the forces of Parliament.

Before the terms could be accepted or refused, however, Captain Stafford, the commanding officer of Wexford Castle, offered to surrender it to the nearest Parliamentarian troops. As the men advanced to take possession of the fortified works, they saw the town open and undefended before them and clambering over the wall flooded into Wexford, seizing the gates and sweeping the surprised defenders before them as they penetrated further into the town, driving a mass of panicked humanity towards the illusory safety of the harbour where many, including Sinnott, leapt into the waters in an effort to escape but were either drowned or shot attempting to flee across the Slaney. All told, an estimated 2,000 of the garrison and inhabitants of Wexford lost their lives during the sack, in comparison with an acknowledged 20 Commonwealth soldiers.

At Drogheda Cromwell had been caught up in the middle of a confused and vicious mêlée when his troops had run amok. At Wexford he was at his headquarters discussing terms for the surrender of the town, and – one assumes – able to exercise command of the army. Yet here he made no attempt to restrain his troops, nor did he move to salvage the hoard of military supplies that he later wrote was one of the reasons for his attempting to take Wexford in the first place. It could be that this inactivity was both a reflection of Cromwell's exasperation at Sinnott's conduct during the surrender negotiations and his contention that by his not having formally offered the town 'quarter', the fate of the inhabitants of Wexford was not his responsibility. If so, then this was a major miscalculation on the part of a man who rarely acted on impulse.

'The Road to Wexford'. Here a body of Coalition cavalry under Sir Thomas Armstrong engage a detachment of Parliamentarian horse in an attempt to defeat them before they can reach the protection of the town. The confused nature of the combat is reflected by the fact that whilst the Parliamentarian troopers are using 'cold steel', a number of the Irishmen are forced to use clubbed pistols as weapons. (Courtesy Seán Ó Brógáin)

**TOP**

Looking out upon King's Channel this perspective from Duncannon Fort gives a good impression of its defensive strength, and indeed, weakness. Whilst Duncannon Fort and Passage Fort remained untaken, their guns could sweep the Barrow estuary and close it to enemy shipping. If one fell, then the other would lose most of its strategic importance. (Kieran Laffan)

**BOTTOM**

This second close-up of Duncannon Fort shows the detail of the eastern-facing wall that protected the landward side of the fort. Here further improvements in fortress design can be seen with the walls now being thicker at the base than at the top and angled slightly to give better protection against enemy fire and mining attempts. Here a small outwork further protects the moat area. (Kieran Laffan)

Despite this, Cromwell's forces did manage to capture a number of small warships as well as a significant amount of artillery and much-needed supplies, although the main prize was a protected harbour that could be used as a base to conduct operations against the Munster coast. The first of these operations was the transfer of Broghill and two regiments of foot (Phayre and Stubber) to the port of Youghal (and thence to Cork) in order to organize and consolidate the anti-Ormond factions within the province whilst Henry Ireton, in preparation for the next stage of the campaign, departed at the head of a large column of troops south-west in an attempt to capture Duncannon Fort on the estuary of the river Barrow in order to unlock the

waterway to Commonwealth warships and thus open the seaborne route to the inland port of Waterford on the river Suir.

Impatient to take the field again and maintain the campaign's momentum, Cromwell gave his troops less than a week before appointing the New Englander George Cooke as governor of Wexford and marching west in an attempt to capture New Ross, an important crossing point on the river Barrow. This new objective was garrisoned by 1,000 men under the command of Sir Lucas Taaffe who, with Ormond vacillating over his campaign objectives, secured permission to surrender on terms as soon as the enemy's heavy artillery had begun to bombard the town walls. Following the established formula, Cromwell deployed his forces about the town and issued a summons for the surrender of New Ross, again citing his continued desire to avoid 'an effusion of blood'.

Taaffe ignored the summons and was soon reinforced by a further 1,500 troops but when the siege guns opened fire on the morning of 19 October he sent a messenger to Cromwell asking for terms. Aware that the weather could break at any moment and whilst hoping to use New Ross as a forward base in which his troops could be put into winter quarters, Cromwell was inclined to leniency but then Taaffe famously raised the subject of the civilian population of the town, asking that any choosing to remain would be permitted to have 'liberty of conscience'.

Perhaps Taaffe's request reminded Cromwell too much of Sinnott's prevarication at Wexford, as his response clearly showed the mailed fist concealed within the velvet glove, reiterating the *only* terms on offer:

> ... what I formerly offered I shall make good. As for your carrying away any artillery or ammunition that you brought not in with you, or hath not come to you since you had command of that place, I must deny you that, expecting that you leave it as you found it. For that which you mention concerning liberty of conscience, I meddle not with any man's conscience. But if by liberty of conscience you mean the liberty to practice the Mass, I judge it best to use plain dealing, and let you know that where the Parliament of England has power, that will not be allowed of ...

This view taken at high tide from the western side of the Barrow Estuary clearly shows the sort of threat that the guns of Duncannon Fort would have posed to Commonwealth shipping. In any event it was the capture of Passage Fort on the western bank that opened the riverine approach to Waterford. (Kieran Laffan)

**LEFT**
This imposing close-up view of one of Waterford's remaining medieval towers clearly shows the thickness of the walls. Considered to be proof against the Parliamentarian field artillery, the defences would have provided scant protection against Cromwell's siege guns, the deployment of which generally heralded the beginning of the end for the defenders. (Kieran Laffan)

**RIGHT**
Part of the remains of Waterford's town walls, the crenellations and arrow slits on this medieval tower clearly show how outdated many towns' defences had become in comparison with the technological advances arising from the advent of gunpowder. (Kieran Laffan)

Cromwell's terms were accepted, but as Taaffe was preparing to evacuate the town one of Inchiquin's Protestant regiments refused to obey orders and instead the men opted to offer their services to Cromwell, an event that was soon followed by news that in Munster Broghill had been doing his work conscientiously – the city of Cork as well as the ports of Kinsale and Bandon had all offered to come to terms with the Commonwealth. For Cromwell, this was a crucial development in the campaign, as not only did the acquisition of these towns further add to Ormond's logistical problems, but they also gave his army the possibility of going into winter quarters in friendly areas, something that would give them a welcome respite from the sickness and disease that had plagued the army since it had moved south from Dublin.

Just as it seemed that Ormond's position had become untenable, on 20 October he received a boost from the fruition of several months' intensive diplomacy – Éoghan 'Rua' Ó Neíll finally agreed to end the infighting and join the Coalition. This accommodation not only added several thousand much needed veteran troops to the order of battle, but also released a significant number of troops which had previously been unable to take the field against Cromwell as they had been assigned to counter any aggressive moves by Ó Neíll.

Moving southwards, and as an outward sign of his earnestness, Ó Neíll sent an advance force of two regiments with a small force of cavalry under Lieutenant-General Richard Farrell to support Ormond; however, instead of continuing towards Munster as agreed, the rest of the army was obliged to halt at Finnea, Co. Cavan, when the veteran commander's health began to fail.

# THE CAMPAIGN FALTERS, WATERFORD, 27 OCTOBER TO 2 DECEMBER 1649

Although Taaffe had managed to bring off most of his garrison intact, the capture of New Ross had increased Cromwell's strategic options by giving him the possibility of either conducting joint operations with Broghill in western Munster, or striking at one of Ormond's last remaining lifelines to the Continent, the inland port of Waterford on the river Suir. Somehow, the Royalist commander had to wrench the tactical initiative from his opponent and breathe new life into the Coalition.

With Farrell now under way with reinforcements from the Ulster Army, Ormond instructed the Earl of Castlehaven to defend the approaches to Waterford by heavily reinforcing the garrison of Duncannon Fort, one of the twin fortifications that protected the Barrow Estuary and whose capture would be a prerequisite for an attempt to take Waterford. (The fort itself guarded the eastern side of the estuary, whilst the approaches from the opposite, western side were guarded by Passage Fort.) On 21 October, Castlehaven oversaw the movement of an additional 2,000 men into the fortress under the command of Colonel Edward Wogan, a former Parliamentarian officer whose determination to succeed in his new command was reinforced by the certain knowledge that, if captured, he would be hanged as a traitor.

The remains of the town wall, near the modern Railway Square, Waterford. The strength of the town lay not in its medieval walls, but in the outlying works at Duncannon Fort and Passage Fort which, holding the Commonwealth Navy at bay, prevented Cromwell from landing his siege artillery until it was too late in the season to make an attempt on the town. (Kieran Laffan)

# Cutting the head off the Hydra, January–June 1650

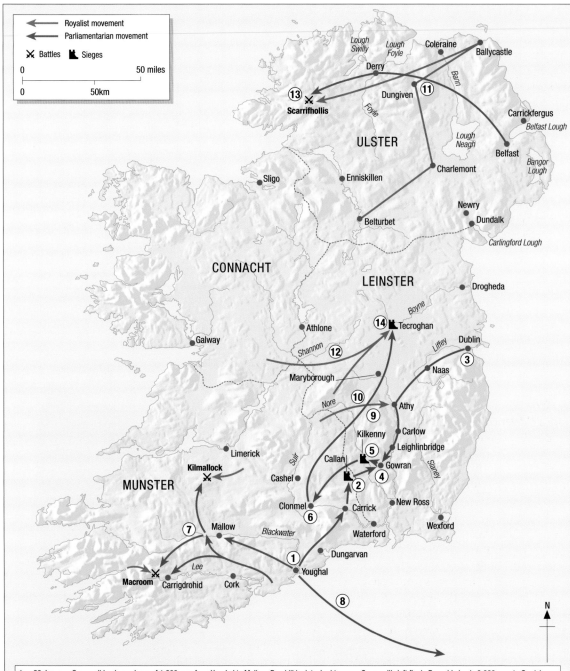

1. 29 January: Cromwell leads a column of 1,200 men from Youghal to Mallow. Broghill is detached to cover Cromwell's left flank. Reynolds leads 3,000 men to Carrick. Ireton follows with army reserve.
2. 3 February: Reynolds begins to reduce Callan's outlying fortifications.
3. 26 February: Hewson leaves Dublin for Callan with 3,000 men.
4. 20 March: the army concentrates at Callan and moves on Kilkenny.
5. 27 March: Kilkenny falls to Parliamentarian forces.
6. 27 April: Cromwell arrives before Clonmel.
7. 10 May: Broghill defeats Irish forces under Roche at Macroom, and subsequently defeats Inchiquin near Kilmallock.
8. 27 May: Cromwell leaves Ireland.
9. May: Reynolds and Hewson move north into Leinster, besieging Tercroghan.
10. May: Castlehaven recaptures Athy.
11. June: MacMahon invades Eastern Ulster, but achieves little and is firced to move west to couenerattack into Donegal by Commonwealth forces under the command of Coote and Venables.
12. 19 June: Clanricarde and Castlehaven combine forces to relieve Tecroghan.
13. 21 June: The Confederate Ulster Army is destroyed by Coote at Scarrifhollis.
14. 25 June: Tecroghan surrenders.

Wogan's defence of Duncannon Fort can, in many ways, be compared to Jones's defence of Dublin prior to the battle of Rathmines. Aggressive, he mounted continuous sorties against the besieging forces, and even when Jones himself arrived with further troops to assume command and the direction of the siege from Ireton, he met with no success. With no suitable landing site for the heavy artillery, which again was being transported by sea, he had no possibility of breaching the fort's modern defences and, even had he been reckless enough to have attempted it, the garrison was too numerous for a successful escalade. Accepting that his task was impossible, on 5 November Jones withdrew and rejoined the main army at New Ross. For the time being, Waterford's outer ring of defences remained intact.

Ormond's confidence soon received a fillip with the arrival of additional troops from Ó Neíll's Army and, acting on intelligence received, detached Inchiquin with 2,500 men to ambush a column of Parliamentarian reinforcements currently en route between Dublin and the new forward base at Wexford, catching up with the English troops several kilometres to the north of their destination. The result was a debacle that in English eyes reaffirmed their superiority over the Irish. With his infantry lagging behind, Inchiquin decided to press on with his cavalry alone in the hope of forcing the outnumbered enemy to halt and deploy for battle, thus allowing the foot to catch up to the main body and deal the Commonwealth troops a decisive blow.

At first the plan worked well, with the Irish horse under Sir Thomas Armstrong successfully repulsing the English troopers; however, ignoring Inchiquin's instructions to pin the enemy, Armstrong launched his men into an uncoordinated pursuit straight into the waiting ranks of Parliamentarian foot who opened formation to allow their horsemen through and then, closing ranks, delivered a well aimed volley at point-blank range that shattered the Irish formation and sent it reeling backwards. With no chance of success, and without orders to conduct operations against Wexford, Inchiquin withdrew once more to the main army.

Any optimism that Ormond may have felt up to this point soon evaporated, not only with the news of the failed ambush but, more importantly, with the confirmation that Ó Neíll had succumbed to his illness and died at Clough Oughter Castle in Co. Cavan on 6 November.

The loss of his erstwhile enemy damaged Ormond's cause on several levels. Not only did it deny him the services of a considerable number of veteran troops, the majority of whom now crucially suspended their participation in the conflict at a time when their involvement could have had a decisive effect, but it also denied him the services of a gifted general who, since his decisive victory over Robert Monro at Benburb in June 1646 and despite his stubborn adherence to the Papal nuncio, had become almost talismanic to a large section of the Catholic population who saw him as the heir to his uncle, Hugh (The Great) Ó Neíll.

Whilst the Royalist high command was considering the impact of these developments, Cromwell struck. Dividing his command in two, he sent Jones and Ireton north with the greater part of the army, to find the enemy and, if possible, bring him to battle. Initially the offensive met with every success, but when Ormond's forces withdrew over the river Nore at Thomastown and destroyed the bridge there, continued operations became unfeasible, leading Jones to pull back to New Ross in order to replenish his supplies.

The only success in this short campaign was the capture of Carrick, a vital crossing point on the river Suir, by a flying column under Reynolds. Not only was the town the 'back door' to Waterford, which could now be approached from the open, western flank, but its possession also established landward communications with Broghill's forces in western Munster. It now became a race to see if Cromwell could exploit the capture of Carrick before Ormond reacted, and, leaving Reynolds with a mixed force of 700 men to garrison the town, the Commonwealth Army passed onto the southern bank of the Suir on 23 November, taking up a position to the west of Waterford a day later.

Unable to catch his adversary, Ormond arrived before Carrick with a small army of almost 4,000 men and promptly decided to split his forces. His Ulster contingent making an ill-prepared assault on the town, whilst he led a number of troops eastwards in an effort to feed some reinforcements into Waterford without interference from Cromwell's forces. The assault on Carrick led by Major Cáthal Geogehan was a catastrophe as the Ulstermen suffered over 500 casualties before conceding defeat and retiring to lick their wounds.

At Waterford, Mayor John Lyvett almost immediately opened negotiations with Cromwell, possibly spurred on by the fact that Jones had recently captured Passage Fort on the western side of the Barrow estuary. The Commonwealth ships standing out to sea, carrying much-needed supplies and above all, Cromwell's siege artillery could now be unloaded a short distance from the English lines.

Whether he was simply playing for time as he later claimed, Lyvett asked for 15 days' grace in which he could discuss the surrender of Waterford with his senior commanders, insisting that during this time the Parliamentarian troops were to make no further approaches to the town walls. Cromwell offered him five days, with the proviso that he accept no further reinforcement from Ormond, and then continued to construct his siege lines.

As talks were going on, the weather broke and with both Cromwell and Jones incapacitated by illness, operations first ground to a halt and then came news that had been long awaited and for just as long dreaded – Ormond had appointed Richard Farrell as military governor of Waterford, reinforcing the garrison with 1,500 veteran Ulster troops. Ever the realist, Cromwell conceded that, for this year at least, the capture of Waterford was impossible and withdrew his army to the port of Dungarvan, sending the men into winter quarters. And it was here, on 10 December, that his campaign suffered a severe setback; exhausted and his body wracked by illness, Jones died and, with his passing, Cromwell lost the most able of his subordinates.

## WINTER QUARTERS

Throughout the remainder of 1649 and on into January 1650 Cromwell threw himself into the resolution of the army's logistical problems with a passion, bombarding both Parliament and the Council of State with demands for money, men and munitions. Sympathetic to the needs of the army in Ireland, Parliament did its best to meet Cromwell's requirements but, as with everything, it took time for new reserves of manpower and *matériel* to be assembled and in the interim Cromwell attempted to raise the army's morale by visiting as many of his outlying garrisons as possible, instructing his principal subordinates to do likewise.

In the opposing camp, the question of morale was also playing deeply on Ormond's mind. He was the head of a coalition that was slowly falling apart, with factionalism threatening to inflict a far greater defeat than had Cromwell. The question was how could he successfully mobilize the support of the Catholic majority and restore Irish fortunes during the coming campaign?

Mounted harquebusier's armour, helmet and bridle gauntlet. Although infantry armour was being gradually phased out, cavalry troopers still wore armour over their buff coats. During the Irish campaign, the protection afforded by body armour often proved decisive against Confederate pistol-armed cavalry. (Courtesy of the Trustees, Royal Armouries, Leeds)

Superficially he was helped by a synod of Catholic bishops that took place at Clonmacoise in early December. After securing his promise to appoint more Catholics to senior command and his acknowledgement of the role of the Catholic clergy in Irish life, the bishops called upon the people to support Ormond, either financially by giving him the means to wage war or by enlisting in the Coalition Army and giving him the manpower to prosecute it.

By late January his army, reinforced not only by drafts from England but also two fresh regiments of troops, Cromwell was once again ready to take the field. In another lightning offensive his plan was to lead a mobile column, supported by Broghill, deep into Munster whilst Ireton and Reynolds would move back across the Suir, striking north at the enemy heartland, their ultimate target being Kilkenny.

On 31 January, Cromwell began offensive operations by leading a force of 1,000 men in a punitive strike towards Mallow before turning back and, in pouring rain, crossing the Suir. Carefully avoiding the garrison at Cahir, he instead continued on to Fethard which he took by a *coup de main* after informing the garrison commander that his force was merely the advance guard of the main Commonwealth Army. The following day, hearing of

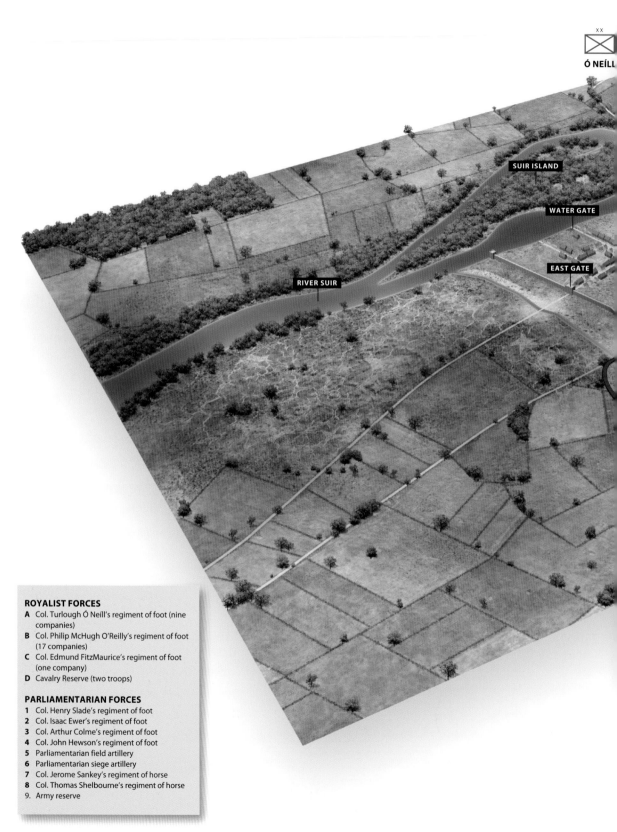

**Ó NEÍLL**

SUIR ISLAND

WATER GATE

EAST GATE

RIVER SUIR

**ROYALIST FORCES**
**A** Col. Turlough Ó Neíll's regiment of foot (nine companies)
**B** Col. Philip McHugh O'Reilly's regiment of foot (17 companies)
**C** Col. Edmund FitzMaurice's regiment of foot (one company)
**D** Cavalry Reserve (two troops)

**PARLIAMENTARIAN FORCES**
**1** Col. Henry Slade's regiment of foot
**2** Col. Isaac Ewer's regiment of foot
**3** Col. Arthur Colme's regiment of foot
**4** Col. John Hewson's regiment of foot
**5** Parliamentarian field artillery
**6** Parliamentarian siege artillery
**7** Col. Jerome Sankey's regiment of horse
**8** Col. Thomas Shelbourne's regiment of horse
9. Army reserve

Note: The base is 2,060 x 1,700m (2,250 x 1,860yds)

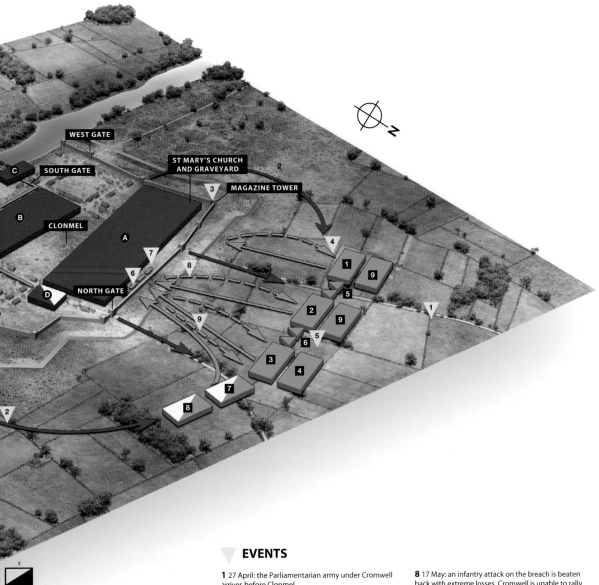

WEST GATE

SOUTH GATE

ST MARY'S CHURCH
AND GRAVEYARD

MAGAZINE TOWER

C

B

CLONMEL

A

D

NORTH GATE

SANKEY

CROMWELL

## ▼ EVENTS

**1** 27 April: the Parliamentarian army under Cromwell arrives before Clonmel.

**2** Ó Neill launches a number of small raids against Parliamentarian positions.

**3** Cromwell bombards the area around St Mary's Church with field cannon, to no effect.

**4** The Parliamentarian assault on St Mary's Church is beaten back with loss.

**5** 15 May: the Parliamentarian siege artillery arrives, and is deployed in battery.

**6** 16 May: the Parliamentarian siege artillery breaches the northern wall of Clonmel. Cromwell plans to assault the breach on the following day, 17 May.

**7** 16 May: Ó Neill constructs interior defence line to contain enemy assault.

**8** 17 May: an infantry attack on the breach is beaten back with extreme losses. Cromwell is unable to rally the troops for a second attack.

**9** 17 May: colonels Sankey and Shelbourne lead their dismounted regiments against the breach. The attack is again beaten off with heavy loss. Cromwell decides to starve the defenders out.

**10** 17 May: whilst John White, Mayor of Clonmel, enters into surrender negotiations with Cromwell, under cover of darkness Ó Neill leads the garrison southwards out of Clonmel towards Waterford.

**11** 18 May: Cromwell despatches a flying column in pursuit of Ó Neill, which only manages to catch up with stragglers and inflicts minimal damage on the retreating column.

# THE SIEGE OF CLONMEL

The events of April/May 1650 showing the movements of the Parliamentarian forces under Oliver Cromwell as they besiege and twice assault the town of Clonmel unsuccessfully.

Clonmel, this interior section of the town's defences clearly shows the buttressed walls and covered walkway that protected the north-eastern part of the town. Commanded by the fortified church itself, this area would prove to be one of the strongest sections of the defences. (Kieran Laffan)

Cromwell's presence in the vicinity, the garrison of Cashel also decamped and the town opened its gates to the triumphant Englishman.

In less than a week Cromwell had not only wrested the strategic initiative from the enemy, but before his opponents could rouse themselves from winter quarters and take the field he had driven a wedge between the Royalist enclaves in Munster and, as Ireton and Reynolds marched north, worse was yet to come. Whilst Ireton brought up the main body of the army, Reynolds rode ahead and captured the town of Callan. Moving up from the west, Cromwell reunited the army and, leaving a small garrison, retraced his steps, intent this time on capturing Cahir, one of the few large towns remaining in enemy hands. Its capture not only serving to isolate the garrisons at Kilkenny and Clonmel, but also to strengthen the lines of communication with Broghill's forces in western Munster.

Confronted by Cromwell's heavy artillery, the garrison of Cahir sought, and were granted, reasonable terms and, with their departure, the jaws of the trap began to close on the remaining Royalist garrisons. With Hewson now moving south from Dublin with 3,000 men and a newly arrived detachment of heavy artillery, Cromwell decided that the time was ripe to move against the enemy capital. With the Royalist forces seemingly paralysed, the columns slowly converged on their objective, purposely offering reasonable terms to any enemy garrisons encountered in a concerted effort to clear their lines of communication before making their final march to their objective.

## THE ARMIES UNITE, KILKENNY, 20–27 MARCH 1650

On 20 March, his small army bolstered by the presence of Hewson's men, Cromwell turned his artillery on the defences of Gowran, the last hurdle on his march to the enemy capital. Initially the garrison commander refused to discuss terms, but despite his later recanting when the walls were breached Cromwell refused to negotiate with him and, addressing the garrison directly, offered the men quarter if they would surrender their officers. Having done

so, they were allowed to march away unarmed but alive, whilst the prisoners were subsequently executed by firing squad.

The road to Kilkenny was now open and, ordering the remainder of his artillery train to be brought up from Fethard, he advanced on the enemy's seat of government. To the north of the town Castlehaven, with a force of 3,000 men, could do nothing but watch as the Parliamentarian troops began to prepare for the attack. Some days earlier he had written to Viscount Dillon asking him to combine their forces for an attack on Cromwell but that worthy, in a repeat of his performance at Rathmines, had refused to stir and a reasonable opportunity to relieve the town was lost.

Dominated to the south by its castle, Ormond's family seat, and separated by the river Nore from its eastern suburb of St John's, the western half of Kilkenny

**THE BITTER PILL OF DEFEAT: CLONMEL, 17 MAY 1650 (pp. 76-77)**

Perhaps overconfident or indeed impatient to bring the campaign to a suitable close in order that he could comply with Parliament's instructions to return to England, Cromwell launched an ill-advised escalade against Clonmel, which was easily beaten off by the defenders. Realizing that the town could be taken only by conventional means, he therefore elected to await the arrival of his siege artillery, which deployed for action on 14 May.

Within two days, a considerable breach had been created in Clonmel's northern wall and Cromwell elected to make a general assault on the morning of 17 May. Hugh 'Dubh' Ó Neíll, in command of the garrison, had not remained idle, during the final bombardment and on the evening of the 16th had begun the construction of a *coupure* or improvised defence work whose function was to funnel any attacking forces into a prepared killing ground where their numerical superiority would not only be negated, but would actually work against them.

His men concealed behind a series of barricades, Ó Neíll allowed the Commonwealth infantry to advance almost to the point of contact and at the last moment the defenders opened fire, scything down ranks of the enemy. Unable to advance into the cauldron of fire, the shattered troops fell back in disarray, swarming over the breach and into the safety of their own lines.

Here we see an extremely agitated Cromwell **(1)** trying to browbeat a number of his fleeing soldiers into rallying for another attack, but to no avail **(2)**. Having lost over a third of the column either dead or wounded the infantry were in no mood to make another attack on Ó Neíll's defences.

Behind Cromwell, colonels Sankey and Shelbourne **(3)** in command of the two divisons of Cromwell's own Regiment of Horse are offering the services of their men to form the next attack wave, confident that the veteran troopers will succeed where the infantry had failed **(4)**.

The dismounted attack went in and reached the Irish barricades but, despite some local success, the Commonwealth troops were again repulsed with significant loss, an estimated total of 3,000 men or almost 40 per cent of Cromwell's Army becoming casualties in the failed assaults.

Running out of ammunition and aware that he could not repulse a fourth enemy attack, Ó Neíll escaped the town under of cover of darkness, adding to Cromwell's frustration at this singular and unaccustomed defeat.

was actually made up of two settlements: 'Irish Town', centred around St Canice's Cathedral, and the much larger 'English Town' (also sometimes referred to as 'High Town'), which had been founded during the 12th century by William Marshal, Earl of Pembroke. Each of the three settlements was covered by its own set of defences and any attack would be comparable to an assault on three separate towns rather than a single urban area.

The governor of Kilkenny, Sir Walter Butler of Powleston – another member of Ormond's extended family, was in a decidedly unenviable position. Over the preceding months, a severe outbreak of plague had not only badly afflicted the civil population but had also decimated his garrison troops. Of the 1,200 men initially placed under his command, almost two-thirds had by this stage succumbed to the disease, leaving him with less than 500 trained soldiers with which to face the besieging army.

Aware that he simply didn't have enough men to defend the entire circuit of the walls, Butler took the only real option available and, opening the town's magazine, attempted to augment his forces by arming as many civilians as possible, deploying his own men to cover English Town and the castle, whilst the new 'militia' were given the task of defending Irish Town and St Johns.

On 22 March, Cromwell initiated the siege with a summons for the town to surrender, writing:

> … my coming hither is to endeavour, if God so please to bless me, the reduction of the city of Kilkenny to their obedience to the State of England, from which by an unheard of massacre of the innocent English, you have endeavoured to rend your selves; and as God hath begun to judge you with his sore plague, so will he follow you until he have destroyed you, if you repent not: Your cause hath been judged already in England, upon them who did abet your evils, what may the principals then expect? By this free dealing you see that I entice you not to a compliance, you may have terms as may save you in your lives, liberties and estates, according to what will be fitting for me to grant, and you to receive; if you choose for the worst, blame your selves: In confidence of the gracious blessing and presence of God with his own cause, which is by many testimonies, I shall hope for a good issue upon my endeavours …

At Kilkenny Cromwell departs from what had been his standard theme – a wish to avoid unnecessary bloodshed. Here, and possibly buoyed by the unparalleled success of his campaign so far or by the fact that he was besieging the enemy capital, he refers for the first time to the Irish Rising of 1641, alluding to Crown collusion in the massacre of the Protestant settlers. Just as importantly, it is also the first occasion in which he identifies himself as an agent of divine will, the first time in which he imbues the conflict in Ireland with religious significance. Butler's immediate response was that he was commanded to '… maintain this city for his majesty, which, by the power of God, I am resolved to do'.

Both sides then settled down to prepare for siege operations and on 24 March Cromwell decided to test the garrison by attacking Kilkenny from opposite sides. Early in the morning, an attempt by Parliamentarian cavalry to storm the North Gate of Irish Town was repulsed with some loss, whilst later in the day he contented himself with occupying St Patrick's Church, which overlooked the town's southern wall and gave him a position from which he could observe Butler's defensive preparations and make his own dispositions accordingly.

# Operations in eastern Munster, February–April 1650

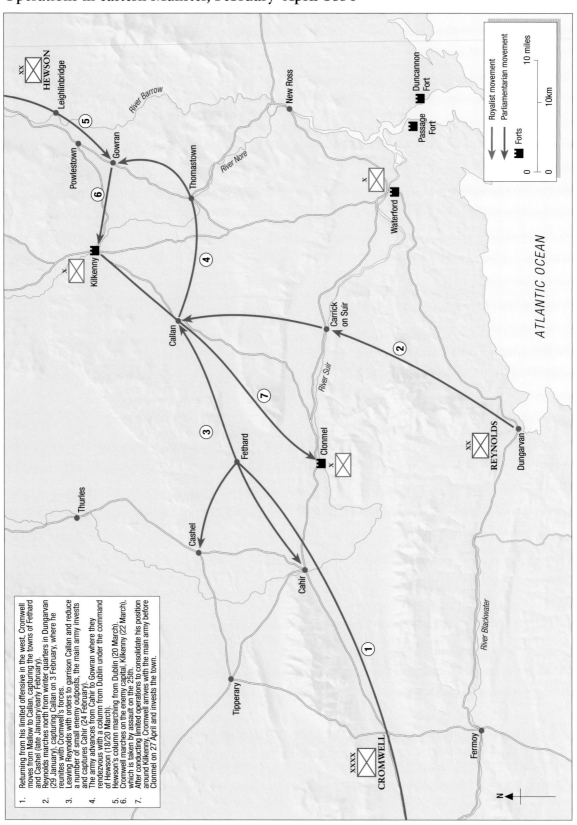

ATLANTIC OCEAN

Royalist movement
Parliamentarian movement
Forts

10 miles
10km

HEWSON
Leighlinbridge
River Barrow
New Ross
Duncannon Fort
Passage Fort
Gowran
Powlestown
Thomastown
River Nore
Waterford
Kilkenny
Callan
Carrick on Suir
River Suir
Thurles
Fethard
Clonmel
REYNOLDS
Dungarvan
Cashel
Cahir
River Blackwater
Tipperary
CROMWELL
Fermoy
N

1. Returning from his limited offensive in the west, Cromwell moves from Mallow to Callan, capturing the towns of Fethard and Cashel (late January/early February).
2. Reynolds marches north from winter quarters in Dungarvan (29 January), capturing Callan on 3 February, where he reunites with Cromwell's forces.
3. Leaving Reynolds with orders to garrison Callan and reduce a number of small enemy outposts, the main army invests and captures Cahir (24 February).
4. The army advances from Cahir to Gowran where they rendezvous with a column from Dublin under the command of Hewson (18/20 March).
5. Hewson's column marching from Dublin (20 March).
6. Cromwell marches on the enemy capital, Kilkenny (22 March), which is taken by assault on the 25th.
7. After conducting limited operations to consolidate his position around Kilkenny, Cromwell arrives with the main army before Clonmel on 27 April and invests the town.

80

Cromwell's plans for the attack were quickly formulated and, sheltered by the imposing bulk of St Patrick's, he established a battery of three heavy cannon which would be able to bombard the town's southern walls unmolested by enemy fire. Aware that the majority of Butler's garrison were untrained he decided to attack again from opposite directions to as to negate the possibility of the threatened sectors being able to support each other. To the north, a force of 1,000 men under the command of Colonel Isaac Ewer would attempt an escalade of Irish Town, whilst in the south, as soon as the siege guns had made a breach, Hewson would lead a storming party against the south wall.

Throughout the morning the cannon battered the walls from close range and, as a section of masonry started to collapse, the gunners intensified their efforts, remorselessly pounding the medieval stonework until the gap gradually widened, providing a rubble-strewn ramp over which the waiting infantry could force their way into the town. As the guns fell silent and the smoke cleared, Cromwell studied the breach and, after a few minutes, gave the signal for the attack.

Sword in hand, Hewson and his deputy, Daniel Axtell, led their men forwards at the run but as they reached the top of the slope they were stopped dead in their tracks by a devastating volley of enemy musketry. Aware that he had no means to counter the enemy bombardment Butler had constructed a series of trenches as a secondary line of defence and packed them with musketeers. Confined by the breach, 30 or so of the attackers – their commanding officer amongst them – went down, and with their front rank decimated, they withdrew in disorder.

Whilst Hewson would later bitterly complain that the signal to attack had been given to soon, Cromwell referred to the failed assault by saying that '… our men upon the signal fell upon the breach, which indeed was not performed with usual courage nor success … indeed it was a mercy to us that we did not farther contend for an entrance there, it being probably that if we had, it would have cost us very dear …'

Conversely Ewer's mission met with complete success for negligible losses. Forcing their way into Irish Town at the cost of three or four casualties, his veteran troops were more than a match for the armed civilians charged with its defence, and were soon in control of the area.

By now painfully aware that English Town would be a hard nut to crack, Cromwell decided to adopt the indirect approach and, on 26 March, ordered Colonel John Gifford to capture the eastern suburb of St John's with a view to seizing the bridge and taking Butler's defences from the rear. Gifford achieved his initial objective with few casualties, but when his forces attempted to storm the bridge they were caught in a crossfire and withdrew with a loss of 50 men.

Despite his having repulsed one enemy assault, the capture of St John's had placed Butler in an impossible position. Simply put, he had too few men to man his defences and, aware that even if he withdrew into Kilkenny Castle, without support from Ormond or Castlehaven, its capture would be only a matter of time, he decided to negotiate a surrender.

Relieved at having taken the town without prohibitive casualties, Cromwell was now prepared to be magnanimous. The garrison, and any civilians who wished to accompany them, was permitted to march out of the town with full honours and a pass of safe conduct, before proceeding to an agreed rendezvous where all weapons, barring an agreed number for personal protection, were to be surrendered.

# SETBACK ON THE SUIR, CLONMEL, 27 APRIL TO 18 MAY 1650

With Kilkenny taken, Cromwell now looked to crown his campaign in eastern Munster with the capture of Clonmel on the river Suir, the sole remaining town of consequence – with the notable exception of Waterford – remaining in enemy hands. But before he could take the field, he needed to reorganize his forces and this unavoidable delay gave the commander of the Clonmel garrison, Major-General Hugh 'Dubh' Ó Neíll an important breathing space in which to prepare the town for the inevitable attack.

Like his uncle, Éoghan 'Rua', a veteran of the Spanish Army of Flanders, Ó Neíll had arrived at Clonmel on 10 December 1649 with two regiments of Ulster foot and, in accordance with Ormond's instructions began to make preparations for the town's defence.

Man and nature had combined to make Clonmel a truly daunting prospect for any potential attacker. To the east and west the six-metre-high walls overlooked low, marshy terrain, whilst the southern wall faced straight on to the deep and fast-flowing Suir. Additionally, and in order to lessen the effect of enemy artillery, the walls on the three 'open' facings were further buttressed on both sides with an escarpment of packed earth and, finally, the northern approach was also covered by a steep ditch to deter enemy mining operations. In effect this meant that the only realistic avenue of approach for a hostile force was from the north, which gave the defending commander the additional advantage of being able to concentrate the bulk of his forces against a single threat.

Despite these obvious advantages, Ó Neíll still had to contend with a number of problems; Clonmel was not only chronically short of supplies but, like Kilkenny, had also suffered heavily from an outbreak of plague, leaving the garrison with at most 2,000 effectives under orders.

After first garrisoning Kilkenny, and then detaching Reynolds with 2,500 men to screen Castlehaven's forces, Cromwell moved south at the head of 9,000 men and 12 field pieces, arriving before the town on 27 April. If, however, he had expected Ó Neíll to wait behind his defences, Cromwell was soon to be disappointed and, despite the cost to his meagre supplies, the Irishman launched a number of blistering attacks on the Commonwealth forces.

Ordinarily the attacking commander would have had the option of simply standing off and allowing hunger and disease to do his work for him, but by this time Cromwell had a strict itinerary. With relations between England and Scotland worsening steadily, it was now obvious to many in the Commonwealth Government that war with the Scots was inevitable. With Sir Thomas Fairfax refusing to assume command of any army sent against the Scots, the next logical choice to many was Cromwell.

Summoned back to England at the beginning of 1650, Cromwell had continually demurred until a suitable compromise was reached that would allow him

Tri-bar lobster pot helmet, English c.1640. Perhaps the most common – and easily recognizable – piece of cavalry headgear is the 'lobster pot'. A refinement upon the 'burgonet'-style helmet is the movable visor with three conjoined bars that allows vision but protects against a slashing attack to the face. (Courtesy of the Trustees, Royal Armouries, Leeds)

to remain in Ireland until such time as he could safely hand over the command to his deputy, Henry Ireton. The agreed point would be the capture of Clonmel, and thus the town needed to be taken without delay. Perhaps this sense of urgency clouded Cromwell's judgement as, having used his light cannon to bombard the north-west sector of the walls around St Mary's Churchyard, he launched an infantry assault against the relatively intact defences, which was inevitably repulsed with loss.

By 16 May, the siege guns were emplaced and had begun to fire upon Clonmel's northern wall. The result was immediate and by late afternoon an extensive breach had been created, both sides being aware that the inevitable assault would go in on the following day. All too aware of his precarious supply situation, Ó Neíll decided to gamble all on a single throw of the dice, his aim being to cause prohibitive casualties on the enemy's attack columns and use the threat of further losses as a bargaining counter in any surrender negotiations.

During the night, work parties began to block off a number of side streets and barricade the lower floors of houses directly behind the breach, creating two narrow channels which would funnel the attacking forces into a specially constructed killing ground or *coupure* some distance further into the town into which he had deployed a large number of troops supported by two light cannon.

At 8.00am on Friday 17 May, the first wave of Cromwell's infantry rushed the breach, clambering across the rubble and into the streets ahead. As the line of troops disappeared from view, a second wave was then given the order to advance.

With his men hidden from enemy sight Ó Neíll waited, biding his time as the redcoats drew ever closer and then, with the pressure from behind pushing the front ranks inexorably forwards, he gave the signal.

The town simply erupted into a cacophony of gunfire as the Irishmen opened a galling fire on the trapped enemy, musket balls raking the packed ranks of Parliamentarian troops at point-blank range. Hit from three sides, the panicked infantry turned and rushed for the relative safety of the breach, leaving over a thousand of their comrades dead and wounded in the narrow streets. Rushing forwards, Cromwell tried to rally the fleeing troops, but the shock of Ó Neíll's ambush had simply been too much for them and they refused to attack again, demanding that the highly paid cavalrymen be sent into the attack. Without hesitation, Colonel Jerome Sankey, commanding one half of Cromwell's double-strength regiment of horse, volunteered his men for the next assault, shortly followed by the commanders of a number of other regiments.

By 3.00pm, the troops were ready and the dismounted troopers advanced at the double, sweeping aside a small number of Ó Neíll's troops who had moved back up to the breach. Forcing their way through the scene of carnage they made their way along the bloody streets and charged the enemy barricade. For a number of hours both sides were locked in combat, the defenders pouring fire into the enemy ranks whilst the cavalrymen tried manfully to hack an opening in the Irish barricade and bludgeon their way into the town. With losses mounting – particularly amongst the officers – the advance had come to a complete standstill, and Sankey saw that there was nothing else for it but to signal the retreat.

For Ó Neíll, the enemy repulse had justified his tactics. The Commonwealth troops had been thrown back with almost 3,000 casualties, but there was a price – not only had he used up virtually all of his supply of powder and shot, but also a large number of his own men had fallen during the intense fighting. Resolving to lead the remainder out of the town under cover of darkness, he then asked the Mayor of Clonmel, John White, to ask Cromwell for terms, hoping to keep the enemy commander busy whilst he made his clandestine escape.

Acutely aware of the damage to his army, and mistakenly believing that Ó Neíll's men would be included within any capitulation, Cromwell acceded to White's request with alacrity and, whilst negotiations began, the Ulstermen crossed the Suir heading for the protection of Waterford. It wasn't until the articles had been signed that Cromwell thought to enquire what Ó Neíll had thought of the surrender, to which White blankly replied that he couldn't answer the question as Ó Neíll was no longer in Clonmel.

Furious, Cromwell immediately sent a party out in pursuit of the fugitives, but although they overtook and killed a number of Ó Neíll's wounded, they were unable to catch up with the main body which, after reaching their destination, was refused entrance by Thomas Preston, the new garrison commander. With no other option available, Ó Neíll ordered his men to disperse into the countryside and make their own way to safety.

Throughout his time in Ireland, Cromwell had pursued his objectives with a single-mindedness that has since been regarded as a manifestation of religious fanaticism. Tactically superior to any of the opponents that he encountered, with the exception of Clonmel he had conducted a model campaign that provided a springboard for operations conducted by his successors.

# THE AFTERMATH

With the surrender of Clonmel, Cromwell handed over command of the army to Ireton, sailing for England on 27 May 1650. As the Irish coast disappeared from view, he is said to have remarked that his sole military setback – the siege of Clonmel – should not be regarded as a military defeat, but rather as a sign from God that should be later, and at length, reflected upon.

Whether he did follow his own advice is unclear as, almost immediately upon his arrival in England, Cromwell was immediately thrown into the planning of the campaign against the Scots that would culminate in the hard-fought victory at Dunbar on 3 September and, as a result, little further mention is made of this episode in his career.

In his 1999 study of the campaign, James Scott Wheeler asserts that Cromwell's departure from Ireland '... removed a source of ruthless energy (from the conflict), and the result would be a decrease in the intensity of operations of the main army under Lord Deputy Ireton ...' Whilst Wheeler is fundamentally correct in his summary of events, what must be considered is that Cromwell's initial aim was to knock the enemy out of the war as the result of a field engagement – indeed this is the accepted rationale for the ratio of cavalry to infantry in the expeditionary force of one: two – whilst with his departure from Ireland, the pace, and indeed the objectives, of the campaign changed dramatically; the earlier policy of seeking a battlefield decision now became subordinated to the necessity of consolidating the military position before the army could conduct further offensive operations.

Fully intent on now bringing the war to a successful conclusion in the face of continued enemy raids throughout the south-east of the country, Ireton elected to oversee personally the reduction of Leinster and its consolidation as a base of future operations, whilst leaving the subjugation of Munster up to Broghill and his principal subordinate, Sir Hardress Waller, who were even then embarking on a deliberate reign of terror that is best exemplified by Broghill's standing orders that all enemy officers captured by his troops were to be executed out of hand without prospect of exchange or ransom. The pursuit of this policy without let or restraint, however heinous it may seem in retrospect, succeeded in its main objective and served to deepen the underlying mistrust between Catholics and Protestants within the enemy ranks, which would ultimately lead to the Catholic clergy ordering the forced expulsion of a significant number of Inchiquin's veterans from the Coalition army on the grounds that they were spiritually unreliable and thus a liability.

Irish Confederate pikeman c.1646–50. Ill equipped in comparison with either his Royalist or Commonwealth contemporaries, the dress and equipment of this soldier are simple in the extreme: a baggy woollen shirt, belted at the waist, tight-fitting trews, soft leather shoes and a woollen cap. For protection he carries a pike with a bodkin head, and a long knife or *sgian*. (Courtesy Seán Ó Brógáin)

# The fall of the Shannon, July 1650–November 1651

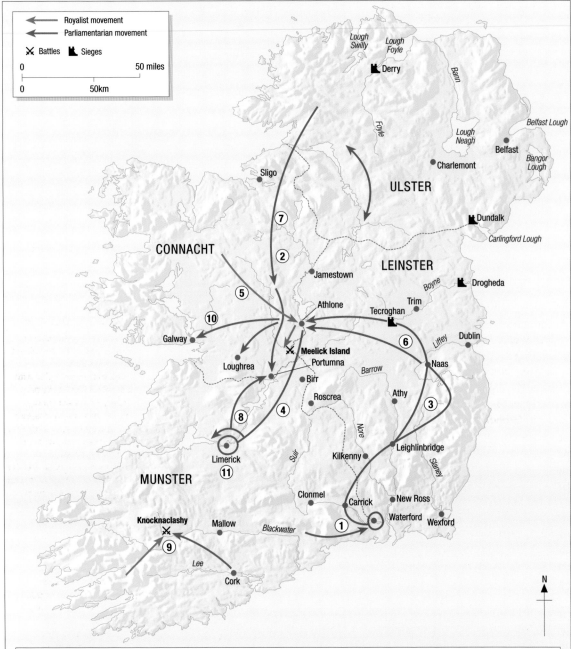

1. Late July 1650: Henry Ireton moves to reinforce the siege of Waterford. With no hope of relief the garrison commander, Thomas Preston, surrenders on 10 August.
2. 14 August: after joint operations with Robert Venables that result in the capture of Charlemont, Sir Charles Coote leads his army south into Connacht in an attempt to capture Athlone from the west.
3. 16 August: Ireton leaves Waterford and marches through Leinster, systematically reducing the remaining Royalist outposts. He continues to Athlone which he reaches on 16 September.
4. 30 September: leaving Coote in command of the besieging forces at Athlone, Ireton moves south along the Shannon in an attempt to take Limerick. An abortive siege is raised on 19 October.
5. October: the Earl of Clanricarde leads the Royalist forces in a counteroffensive to relieve pressure on Athlone. Despite initial success Axtell heavily defeats him at Meelick Island on 21 October. Parliamentarian forces subsequently withdraw into winter quarters.
6. February 1651: Hewson leads a punitive raid to reduce Royalist outposts in Westmeath and secure the approaches to Athlone.
7. 3 June: Ireton crosses the Shannon to operate against enemy positions in western Connacht, occupying O'Brienbridge and covering the approaches to both Athlone and Limerick, placing the latter under siege.
8. June: Sir Charles Coote again marches south into Connacht and in conjunction with Ireton's troops invests Athlone, which surrenders on 18 June.
9. 22 June: Broghill heavily defeats Royalist forces under Viscount Muskerry at Knocknaclashy. A running campaign begins in which Broghill effectively neutralizes Royalist forces in western Munster.
10. July: Coote marches west against Galway which remains under siege until May 1652.
11. 27 October: faced with civilian unrest and dissent amongst the garrison, the governor of Limerick, Hugh 'Dubh' Ó Neíll, surrenders the city to Ireton, effectively marking the end of formal military operations.

Although the forces under his command had by now increased to almost 30,000 men, and with the greater proportion of these either sick or in garrison, the number actually available to Ireton for service in the coming campaign was significantly less and thus his objectives for the coming year had to be more realistic and attainable. Conversely, within the enemy ranks, and despite the significant loss of manpower caused by the pacification of Munster and the enforced catholicization of the army, Ormond could still call upon the services of upwards of 20,000 men divided between the various provincial armies and so, at least in numerical terms, the 1650 campaign would begin with both sides enjoying some form of parity.

Towards the end of May, Ormond uncharacteristically went over to the offensive and made an attempt to break the Commonwealth siege of Tecroghan. Although some of the Irish troops managed to fight their way through the enemy lines and reinforce the garrison before the main army was forced to withdraw, the main result of the action was the development of a feud between Clanricarde and Castlehaven, each of whom blamed the other for their failure to achieve their objectives and which if left to fester, threatened to destroy the Coalition from within. As if this were not bad enough, Ormond soon received calamitous news from the North.

In the mistaken belief that the local population would support him by rising up against their Commonwealth garrisons, the Confederates' Ulster Army under Bishop Heber MacMahon had launched an ill-prepared and

Reconstruction of a Confederate cavalry cornet c.1649. Unlike infantry colours, which often followed a religious theme coupled with a declaration of loyalty to the Crown, the smaller cavalry cornets invariably displayed a more personal armorial device, in this instance an armoured arm casting a spear from heaven, an allegory for a 'divine thunderbolt'. (Courtesy of Seán Ó Brógáin/Cavan Museum)

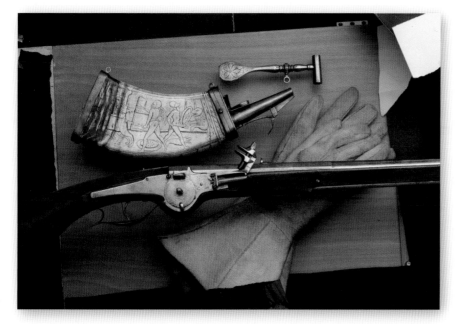

A trooper's equipment. Detail of a wheellock carbine, spanning key, powder flask and buff gauntlets of a Parliamentarian dragoon. Attached by means of a sling attached to the carbine's forestock and butt, these weapons could be carried slung over the shoulder and were a perfect interim solution to the provision of firearms for mounted infantry, having few of the disadvantages of the more common matchlock musket. (Courtesy of the Trustees, Royal Armouries, Leeds)

Matchlock military musket, English c.1640. Named after its firing mechanism, whereby a lit cord or 'match' ignited the charge, this most common of infantry firearms could also double as a club in hand-to-hand combat. (Courtesy of the Trustees, Royal Armouries, Leeds)

inconclusive offensive into eastern Ulster and, despite some minor initial successes, it had subsequently withdrawn westwards into Donegal where, pursued by Commonwealth forces under Coote and Venables, it was brought to battle on 21 June at Scarrifhollis on the outskirts of Letterkenny. Despite enjoying superiority of numbers and the advantage of terrain, MacMahon decided to ignore his senior officers' advice and, moving down from the high ground, fight an offensive battle. The result was a disaster for the Confederates who, deployed in an unwieldy mass, were simply unable to counter the smaller and more flexible enemy units who, having pushed back the Irish advance guard, simply advanced to within small-arms range and poured volley after volley of fire into the Irish ranks until the Ulstermen, the rump of Ó Neíll's proud army, broke and were destroyed in a series of small running engagements.

Although MacMahon had managed to escape from the confusion of the battlefield, Coote now decided to emulate Broghill by ordering the execution of a number of captured enemy officers – including Colonel Henry Ó Neíll, son of Éoghan 'Rua' – who had already been given parole in return for their surrender.

The militant bishop would not long survive his defeat, being captured and hanged at Enniskillen some days after the battle and, with his execution, the fighting in Ulster, like that in Munster, came to a virtual end, the focus of the war now shifting inexorably to the line of the Shannon.

With the fall of Tecroghan on 25 June, Ireton could now afford to send forces against Athlone, whilst he himself moved to reduce Waterford. Although the town's garrison had successfully defied Cromwell, sickness and disease had by now reduced it to less than 700 effectives and, with his stocks of powder and ammunition now almost nonexistent, its commander Thomas Preston – who had recently been ennobled by Charles II as Viscount Tara – was obliged to capitulate on whatever terms he could obtain. Articles of surrender were signed on 10 August and, their position now isolated and further resistance meaningless, the garrison of Duncannon Fort soon followed suit.

Following his victory at Scarrifhollis, and with Venables deployed to cover his lines of communications, Coote now marched southwards, laying siege to the fortress of Charlemont, the last remaining Coalition stronghold in Ulster. Commanded by Sir Phelim Ó Neíll, the town was protected by perhaps the most modern defensive works in Ireland and was therefore regarded as being a difficult proposition for any attacking force. Understandably, an initial summons for the fortress to surrender fell on deaf ears, and Coote's heavy artillery proceeded to bombard the defences for several days before the walls were breached on 7 August.

The following day, and in a move reminiscent of his kinsman's defence of Clonmel, Ó Neíll gathered his remaining troops together and, as the attacking column clambered over the rubble, led his men forwards in a desperate and bloody counterattack that threw the enemy back at a cost of almost 1,000 casualties. With supplies now dwindling and with many of his original garrison now dead or severely wounded, Ó Neíll could only sit and anxiously wait for Coote's next move but after a week of further inactivity and perhaps unwilling to risk prohibitive losses, the Commonwealth commander sent a messenger to Ó Neíll, offering the defenders of Charlemont the full honours of war, allowing them to march away with arms and baggage to the nearest Coalition positions.

For the Catholic clergy, which was to all intents and purposes the driving force behind the Coalition, these successive defeats were the final straw, and it was unanimously decided that Ormond should be replaced as commander-in-chief of the Coalition forces. The earl refused to submit to the ecclesiastical pressure and the bishops then threatened any Catholic who served under Ormond with excommunication, whilst simultaneously promoting Clanricarde as a suitable replacement.

Whilst the enemy high command tore itself apart, Ireton continued with his campaign of consolidation, initially sending Waller to invest Limerick and then, leaving Broghill to consolidate the Parliamentarian hold on Munster, taking the rest of the army north towards Naas, before turning west and advancing on Athlone which was reached on 16 September, uniting his forces with those of Coote who had moved to secure the Shannon crossings after the fall of Charlemont.

Masking Athlone, Ireton continued south to Limerick in an attempt to take it quickly, but the city refused a summons to surrender on 6 October. Until now, Ireton had followed his own council, but now he called a meeting of senior officers to canvass their opinions and was told that the siege should be immediately raised and the army sent into winter quarters.

Preoccupied with Limerick, Ireton was in no position to deal with Clanricarde's sudden offensive aimed at breaking the siege of Athlone. Crossing the Shannon south of the town, the Irishmen met with initial success, but as increasing numbers of enemy troops took the field against him Clanricarde was forced to withdraw to a defensive position on Meelick Island in the Shannon.

Attacking on the night of 25 October, Commonwealth forces under Axtell secured a foothold on the island, but were unable to dislodge the Connachtmen and, as day broke, Axtell offered the remaining defenders quarter having them killed out of hand as soon as they had been disarmed and secured. It was a disaster for the Irish who in less than two months had seen two of their three main field armies annihilated by the enemy.

On 6 December 1650, Ormond bowed to the inevitable and, having endorsed Clanricarde as his successor, left Ireland to go into exile in France to be followed afterwards by Inchiquin and a number of other senior Protestant officers who had all sought personal terms from Parliament.

With the campaigning season at a close, both commanders turned their minds to other matters. Ireton launching a number of punitive raids into the countryside aimed at countering the increasing depredations of Irish irregulars or 'Tories', whilst Clanricarde not only attempted to heal the rift caused by the acrimony at Tecroghan, but also had to deal with the ambitions of Duke Charles of Lorraine who, in return for the title 'Protector of Ireland', was apparently willing to lead several thousand veteran mercenaries to Ireland and assume overall command of the Coalition forces. Exactly how Lorraine intended to avoid Commonwealth naval patrols and land his troops in Ireland will always remain unclear but after permission was refused for him to embark his troops from Spanish ports, Clanricarde subsequently repudiated the negotiations and the agreement fell apart.

With time on his side, Ireton waited until there was more than sufficient grazing for his horses before beginning his operations for 1651. For the first time enjoying a massive numerical superiority, his plan was for Coote to feint southwards from Ulster and, when the Irish had moved to counter the threat, for the main army to move against both Athlone and Limerick. Clanricarde took the bait and, leaving Castlehaven to cover the Shannon, hastened north to check Coote's advance.

On reaching the Shannon, Ireton simply bypassed Castlehaven and, bridging the river, sent Reynolds north to turn the Irish position, a position that had become more untenable on 18 June when Athlone surrendered to Hewson, reinforced by Coote who had simply swept Clanricarde aside. The army now had a direct supply line to Dublin and Ireton could now contemplate besieging Limerick, whilst detaching troops to cover the enemy forces in western Galway. By 14 June, his preparations were complete and the city summoned to surrender, a demand that Hugh 'Dubh' Ó Neíll, in command of the garrison, refused. With Broghill ably defeating a relief attempt by Viscount Muskerry at Mallow, the scene was now set for the final act of the war.

With a number of attempts to take the city by escalade repulsed with heavy loss, Ireton now contented himself with letting hunger and disease do his work for him, gradually tightening his siege lines to render attempt at either breakout or relief impossible. Cut off from the outside world, Ó Neíll's only option was to try to drag matters out, stalling at the negotiating table in the hope that the weather would deteriorate and force Ireton to send his troops early into winter quarters as he had the previous autumn. Constant skirmishing took place as the defenders sallied out against enemy patrols or work parties, but whilst the enemy could replace his losses with ease, this constant attrition only served to weaken Ó Neíll's position within the city and it soon became clear that Ireton had no intention of raising the siege.

By the end of September dissent had begun to reach dangerous levels, but with the support of the clergy Ó Neíll managed to maintain a tenuous control over the city. Matters came to a head in October when Commonwealth artillery finally breached the city walls and many, including some members of the garrison, felt that terms should be sought before Ireton could order a general assault.

Lieutenant-Colonel Fennell, who had earlier been accused of attempting to deliver Clonmel to Cromwell, now seized one of the city gates and turned its guns inwards against the garrison. The message was plain, either Ó Neíll treated with the enemy or Ireton would be invited in. In any event, at a cost of several thousand lives the siege of Limerick was effectively over.

In victory, Ireton would prove merciless. Although Ó Neíll himself avoided the death sentence through the auspices of the Spanish ambassador, many of his senior subordinates – including Fennell – were tried and executed by the victors. Almost a month to the day after his victory, Ireton died, succumbing to the disease that had so plagued the Commonwealth forces since their arrival in Ireland, and although Galway would hold out against the besieging forces for another six months, the war was entering its final stages with a campaign being waged against increasing numbers of Irish irregulars who were conducting guerilla operations against Commonwealth outposts and lines of supply.

Eventually, senior officers such as Preston would be permitted to take their troops and enter into foreign service, thus removing a possible focus for continued resistance or discontent, leaving the country to be carved up by the Commonwealth commissioners following in the army's wake.

# THE BATTLEFIELDS TODAY

Despite its relatively short duration the sheer scale of the campaign means that many towns are able to claim some form of link with the fighting in 1649–50. These range in scope from battle sites to sieges or indeed to areas where the Commonwealth forces may have encamped during the course of the campaign. A good idea is, time permitting, to follow the route of Cromwell's advance either in a campaign or a local context such as the Boyne Valley or the Kilkenny–Clonmel–Waterford area, as such an approach is often useful in giving the student an inkling of the original commander's perspective.

Following Michael Jones's victory at Rathmines, the site of which has since become an unfortunate casualty of urban expansion, Cromwell's initial plan of operations was based upon the capture of three strategic towns, namely Drogheda, Wexford and Waterford, all of which are certainly worth a visit, providing an evocative backdrop to any study of the campaign both in terms of historical remains or through local museums such as the Mill Mount in Drogheda, which is based in a restored Martello tower built during the 19th century on the position of Aston's final headquarters, and therefore the site of the darkest hour in the town's history.

Kilkenny Castle. Remodelled by Ormond in 1661, and presented to the Irish nation in 1967 by James Arthur Butler, 6th Marquess and 24th Earl of Ormond, Kilkenny Castle is a prime example of the work of government bodies in restoring and maintaining sites associated with the Cromwellian conquest. Now managed by the Irish Office of Public Works, the castle is not only open to the general public but is also home to the Butler Gallery of Contemporary Art. (Image courtesy and copyright, the Office of Public Works, Ireland)

Other towns such as Cahir, Fethard or New Ross, whose capture formed the framework upon which Cromwell based his entire strategic planning and on which the Commonwealth forces later established their control over the countryside, are also worth visiting, in particular Fethard, which still boasts a complete circuit of medieval walls. The Irish countryside is literally studded with castles and towers the majority of which figured during the Irish Rising of 1641, the Confederate War and the Cromwellian conquest; it would take another book of this size simply to list them all.

Each town or castle, whether great or small or whether taken by storm or *coup de main* has its own story to tell and it is fitting to note that, on both a local and a national level, both the British and Irish governments are actively working to preserve these important monuments for future generations. Suggested sites of interest can be contacted as follows:

Duncannon Fort,
Duncannon,
New Ross,
Co. Wexford,
Ireland
Tel:     00 353 51 389454
Email:  info@duncannonfort.com
Net:     www.duncannonfort.com


Mill Mount Museum,
The Governor's House,
Millmount,
Drogheda,
Co. Louth,
Ireland
Tel:     00 353 41 9833097
Fax:     00 353 41 9841599
Net:     www.millmount.net

Cavan County Museum,
Virginia Road,
Ballyjamesduff,
Co. Cavan,
Ireland
Tel:     00 353 49 8544070
Fax:     00 353 49 8544332
Email:  ccmuseum@eircom.net
Net:     www.cavanmuseum.ie

Kilkenny Castle,
The Parade,
Kilkenny City,
Co. Kilkenny,
Ireland
Tel:     00 353 56 7704100
Fax:     00 353 56 7704116
Net:     www.kilkennycastle.ie

# BIBLIOGRAPHY

Any study of the Cromwellian conquest of Ireland and its aftermath needs to encompass both contemporary and modern works, each with its distinct perspective on the conflict and individual events, and the following list enumerates the various titles consulted in the preparation of this work.

The Internet is also a great aid to research and a special mention should also be made of two online services which have greatly facilitated the research for this book – 'C.E.L.T.' (The Corpus of Electronic Texts) which is run by University College, Cork and 'Google Books' both of which have scanned a considerable number of contemporary manuscripts and publications from a number of museums and trusts worldwide.

Asquith, Stuart, Men-at-Arms 110: *The New Model Army, 1645–60* Osprey Publishing Ltd: Oxford, 1981

Barnard, T. C., *Cromwellian Ireland – English Government and Reform in Ireland 1649–1660* The Clarendon Press: Oxford, 2000

Berresford Ellis, Peter, *Hell or Connaught – The Cromwellian Colonization of Ireland 1652–1660* St Martin's Press: New York, 1975

Carlyle, Thomas, *Cromwell's Letters and Speeches* Ward Lock: London, 1846

Castlehaven, James Touchet, *The Earl of Castlehaven's Memoirs or His Review of the Civil Wars in Ireland: With his Own Engagement and Conduct Therein* Charles Broome: London, 1684

Casway, Jerrold I., *Owen Roe O'Neill and the Struggle for Catholic Ireland* University of Pennsylvania Press: Philadelphia, 1984

Ferguson, Kenneth, 'Contemporary accounts of the battle of Rathmines, 1649' *Irish Sword*, Vol. XXI, No. 86 (Winter 1999)

Gardner, Samuel R., *History of the Great Civil War* four vols, Windrush Press: London, 1987

——, *History of the Commonwealth and Protectorate* four vols, Windrush Press: Adlestrop, 1988

Gentles, Ian, *The New Model Army in England, Ireland & Scotland, 1645–1653* Blackwell Publishers: Oxford, 1992

Gilbert, Sir John T. (ed), *A Contemporary History of Affairs in Ireland, from AD 1641 to 1650, with an Appendix of Original Letters and Documents* three vols, Irish Archaeological & Celtic Society: Dublin, 1879–80

Harrington, Peter, Fortress 9: *English Civil War Fortifications 1642–51* Osprey Publishing Ltd: Oxford, 2003

Henry, Chris, New Vanguard 108: *English Civil War Artillery 1642–51* Osprey Publishing Ltd: Oxford, 2005

Kenyon, John & Ohlmeyer, Jane, (eds.) *The Civil Wars – A Military History of England, Scotland and Ireland 1638–1660* Oxford University Press: Oxford, 1998

Kerr, Archibald, *An Ironside of Ireland* Heath Cranton: London, 1923

Kitson, Sir Frank, *Prince Rupert – Portrait of a Soldier* Constable & Co.: London, 1994

——, *Prince Rupert – Admiral and General-at-Sea* Constable & Co.: London, 1998

——, *Old Ironsides – The Military Biography of Oliver Cromwell* Weidenfeld & Nicholson: London, 2004

Larcom, Thomas A., *History of the Cromwellian Survey of Ireland, AD 1655–6* Irish Archaeological Society: Dublin, 1881

Lenihan, Pádraig, *Confederate Catholics at War 1641–49* Cork University Press: Cork, 2001

McKeiver, Philip, *A New History of Cromwell's Irish Campaign* Advance Press: Manchester, 2007

Murphy, Rev. Denis S. J., *Cromwell in Ireland* M. H. Gill & Son: Dublin, 1897

Ó Cahán, T. S., *Owen Roe O'Neill* T. Joseph Keane & Co: London, 1968

Ó Siochrú, Micheál, *God's Executioner – Oliver Cromwell and the Conquest of Ireland* Faber & Faber: London, 2008

Ohlmeyer, Jane, *Civil War and Restoration in the Three Stuart Kingdoms* Four Courts Press: Dublin, 2001

—— (ed.), *Ireland from Independence to Occupation 1641–1660* Cambridge University Press: Cambridge, 1995

Reilly, Tom, *Cromwell at Drogheda* Broin Print Limited: Drogheda, 1993

——, *Cromwell – An Honourable Enemy* Phoenix Press: London, 1999

Roberts, Keith, Elite 25: *Soldiers of the English Civil War (1) – Infantry* Osprey Publishing Ltd: Oxford 1992

——, Warrior 43: *Matchlock Musketeer 1588–1688* Osprey Publishing Ltd: Oxford 2002

——, *Cromwell's War Machine – The New Model Army 1645–1660* Pen & Sword: Barnsley 2005

Ryder, Ian, *An English Army for Ireland* Partizan Press: Southend, 1987

Spencer, Charles, *Prince Rupert, The Last Cavalier* Weidenfeld & Nicholson: London, 2007

Tincey, John, Elite 27: *Soldiers of the English Civil War (2) – Cavalry* Osprey Publishing Ltd: Oxford, 1993

——, Warrior 44: *Ironsides: English Cavalry 1588–1688* Osprey Publishing Ltd: Oxford, 2002

Wedgewood, Cicely V., *The Trial of King Charles I* Wm. Collins Sons & Co.: London, 1964

Wheeler, James Scott, *Cromwell in Ireland* Gill & Macmillan: Dublin, 1999

——, *The Irish & British Wars 1637–1654: Triumph, Tragedy and Failure* Routledge: London, 2002

Young, Peter, Men-at-Arms 14: *The English Civil War Armies* Osprey Publishing Ltd: London, 1995

# INDEX

Figures in **bold** refer to illustrations.